THE
BUSINESS OF
Fashion

LINDA DREW

THE BUSINESS OF

Fashion

CAMBRIDGE
UNIVERSITY PRESS

Published by the Press Syndicate of the University of Cambridge
The Pitt Building, Trumpington Street, Cambridge CB2 1RP
40 West 20th Street, New York, NY 10011-4211, USA
10 Stamford Road, Oakleigh, Victoria 3166, Australia

First published 1992

Printed in Great Britain by
Ebenezer Baylis & Son Ltd, The Trinity Press, Worcester, and London

A catalogue record for this book is available from the British Library

ISBN 0 521 40825 3 paperback

Cover illustration by Nicky Dupays

GO

Contents

My thanks are due to the London Institute Library (Back Hill and Leicester Square), Top Shop buying department, Gill Dale, Josephine Collins, Geoff Moore and Naomi Jamieson for much practical help and direction.

INTRODUCTION

The main purpose of this book is to provide an introduction to the theory and practice of marketing in the fashion industry. It is aimed primarily at students of fashion and textiles who are specialising in the production, marketing and retailing of fashion goods. It is also intended for those who are already involved in the fashion business, to enable them to widen and update their knowledge of current working practices, and for those who just want to know more about the fashion world and how it functions.

Each chapter has relevant and stimulating illustrations which stress the very visual aspects of the business of fashion. The many references to the various qualities of the fashion product emphasise the fact that thorough knowledge of the merchandise is the key to making correct business decisions.

There are review assignments at the end of most chapters which can be used by the reader to assess how much has been learned. They also provide practice in some of the skills required in the fashion world, such as visual awareness and discrimination, communication and, of course, business sense. There is also a useful reference section at the end of the book with suggestions for further reading.

Whatever the intention of the reader, this book should prove enjoyable and informative reading, whether it is used just for reference or read from cover to cover.

Chapter 1

THE NATURE OF FASHION

This close-fitting silhouette of the 1950s emphasises the feminine qualities and shape of the wearer.

'**Fashion:** a style in clothes, cosmetics, behaviour, etc., especially the latest or most admired style'

This dictionary definition implies, by the use of the word 'latest', that fashion is constantly changing but it does not tell us what it takes for something to be regarded as fashionable, except that it is the 'most admired'. In other words, for something to be accepted as fashionable, a significant number of people have to acknowledge it as such and give at least minimal signs of approval. But how does the style emerge in the first place? Clearly it does not appear overnight. In this chapter, and in Chapters 2 and 3, we shall be looking at how and why certain styles develop and change.

Fashion is evolutionary

Basic fashion shapes (silhouettes) originate from the desire to emphasise or deny the natural form. Some silhouettes are close-fitting, following the natural curves of the body, while others may be loose-fitting with a shape that is almost independent of the form underneath. Most fall somewhere in between: close-fitting in some areas and loose in others.

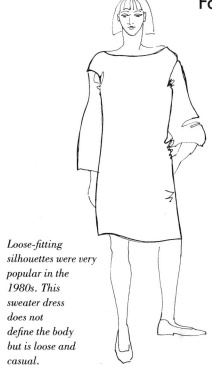

Loose-fitting silhouettes were very popular in the 1980s. This sweater dress does not define the body but is loose and casual.

Fashion styles are based on silhouettes with variations in details such as skirt length, types of trimming, and so on. A style emerges and then changes gradually, in response to influences in the world at large which we shall examine later in this chapter. It eventually disappears but not before it has become extreme, with certain features accentuated until the overall appearance is cheap and vulgar and is unacceptable to most consumers. The style is then dropped in favour of a new one which will, by then, be emerging.

A style emerges and then changes gradually, in response to influences in the world at large which we shall examine later in this chapter. It eventually disappears but not before it has become extreme, with certain features accentuated until the overall appearance is cheap and vulgar and is unacceptable to most consumers. The style is then dropped in favour of a new one which will, by then, be emerging.

There is obviously a limit to the number of possible silhouettes and to the variations of styles based on them, so styles tend to be regenerated at intervals, although the length of time between an original and a repeat may be many years.

The de-emphasised 'Empire line' silhouette of the early nineteenth century, which concentrated on height, elegance and clean lines rather than trim and shape.

This evening ensemble from 1911 shows an uncluttered and clean silhouette, which is very reminiscent of the 'Empire line' of the early nineteenth century. Even the accessories have a similar theme.

LONDON FULL & HALF DRESS.

The fashion cycle

Fashion cycles can be identified in much the same way as product life cycles have been identified by marketing theorists. The theory that fashion is a cyclical thing has been the subject of much debate, as the word 'cycle' implies that a fashion will 'come in' and 'go out' in a regular way, but this is not so. Fashion cycles can best be shown in the form of a graph.

The graphs show three different types of fashion cycle, all of which have the same basic stages.

The fashion cycle: a fad. The fad garment or style sells very fast in the introduction and rise stages, peaks very quickly and declines without trace, usually within one season.

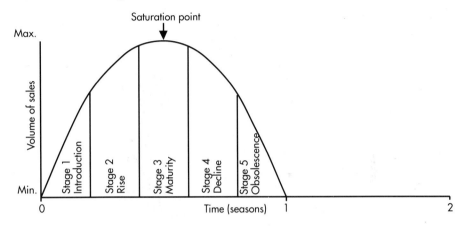

The fashion cycle: a classic. The classic garment or style will have been introduced as a practical or functional garment and stays permanently in the maturity stage.

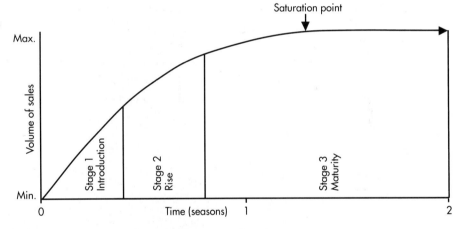

The fashion cycle: a standard trend. The standard trend garment or style takes some time to be accepted through stages 1–3 and declines faster than it rises. This graph shows the standard trend declining into obsolescence after two seasons. In practice, however, sales may continue well beyond this period.

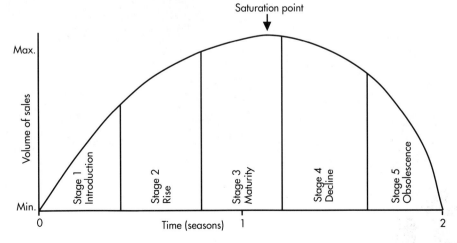

The introduction

This is the first stage where **fashion active** consumers are first introduced to a new style. Certain **style leaders** and **early accepters** will pioneer the wearing of that style. Others will watch with interest (and some with incredulity!).

The rise

By the second stage, the style has had a little more publicity. Style leaders have worn it, and it may have made fashion headlines in the press. **Fashion followers** will then pick up the style in versions that are cheaper and a little less extreme.

Maturity

The peak of the maturity stage is known as the saturation point. This is where the majority of consumers have accepted the style in an even more modified form and at a price to suit them. These **fashion average** consumers will shop in large multiples or variety chains and they will not worry about the lack of exclusiveness. By this stage, the fashion active consumer may well have dropped the style.

The decline

Although people are still wearing the style, it has become much less interesting due to overexposure. This is when a lot of stores will either mark the price down or offer a discount on the style so that what stock is left can be sold quickly. People with less money or less style-consciousness, due either to age or socio-economic concerns, will adopt the style at this stage. These people are known as **decline laggards** or **fashion reactive**, as they are slow to react to changes in fashion.

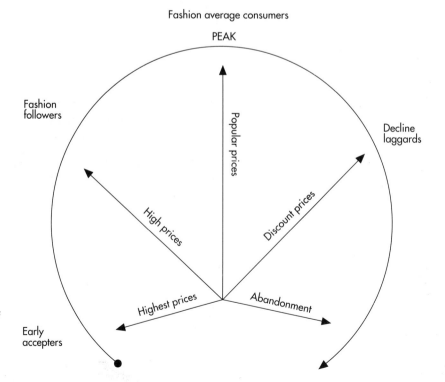

Different types of consumer buy fashion goods at specific stages of the fashion cycle, according to price.

Obsolescence

The last, and most embarrassing stage is when most people look at the style and express near physical distaste for it: 'Yuk! You couldn't pay me to wear that!' The style, at this stage, is often far removed from the original version, being vulgar, cheap or poorly made. It is no wonder, then, that the style can remain obsolete for many years. In fast-moving fashion stores there is an element of planned obsolescence. The store's buyers will know that certain styles carry faddish elements which will destine them for the sale bin, in much the same way as a carton of milk has a 'consume by' date.

Standard trend cycle

The trend cycle is probably the most complex. For a whole style to be regenerated it has to have become inappropriate for the generation who originally bought it. Someone might say: 'Oh look! My mum used to wear dresses like that. I've seen them in pictures in the family album'. But mum, now many years older, is unlikely to readopt the style because it is unsuitable for her present lifestyle. This type of styling is known as **retro**, where even the music and media of an age can be revived, too. The more common form of regeneration is where a person moves from one target consumer bracket to the next and a style they used to wear comes back in time to be worn by their younger brothers or sisters.

Of course, a style never returns in exactly the same way, as technology and society have always moved on, too. It may take five to fifteen years for a style to be regenerated and, when it is considered 'in' fashion again, many versions will be made of it, in different fabrics and colours and with different trims, until the style is exhausted or until it has reached saturation point.

Classic cycle

This is really a misnomer! A classic really never dates and therefore never needs to be regenerated, although, of course, there are times when certain classics are more popular than others because they complement trends. Most classics were designed to satisfy practical and functional clothing requirements, so it is not surprising to find that many of them were originally introduced as workwear or uniforms. Good examples are trench coats, men's white shirts, knitted cardigans, bomber jackets and Argyll socks. These classics are often known as the 'bread and butter' of fashion.

Fad cycle

Another misnomer, but curiously this is a type of style which is so transient that it often eludes description. Fads are most often found, in the first instance, in accessories or in smaller items that are reasonably cheap. There is usually a gimmick or humorous element to a fad. It is this element that makes us want to buy it: 'Look! Sequinned hotpants! Deely-boppers! A puffball skirt!' Like most jokes, the humour is short lived, and tends to be most prevalent in the 'silly seasons' of the year, the times when we are most susceptible to being frivolous or jokey. Holiday, high summer and Christmas are the best times. How many photographs have you of yourself or friends in silly T-shirts on a beach, or with outrageous earrings at a New Year party? Everybody has style encounters they would rather forget. They are usually with fads, and at times when they are less inhibited and more likely to buy for fun. It is mainly large multiple fashion stores that will risk stocking many faddish items, because the risk element is high and therefore more threatening to the profits of the smaller store.

Fashion cycles can be used as an aid to fashion prediction, but there are no hard and fast rules so, to understand how fashion can be predicted and how it moves generally, it is better to proceed and look at other elements of the business of fashion.

Why fashion changes

Because our desire for newness never ceases, our quest for new things, new environments, and new visual stimuli is continuous. Try to remember the last time you changed your living room around, or bought new clothes. Were your reasons for doing so solely practical? Inevitably, the answer is sometimes 'yes' – your jeans or trainers can literally wear out. Ballgowns, on the other hand, very rarely do; they are replaced after considerably less wear. This is because people have a very real need for changing visual stimuli: children who are constantly given bright and interesting playthings will grow up to be inquisitive and demanding young people; if deprived of colour, texture, sound and interesting activities, they can become dull, listless and quiet. So, by constantly changing what we wear, we change our environment and satisfy a basic need, not only in ourselves but in those who know or meet us.

However, this human desire for change is only one of the reasons why people change the way they dress. Some fashion theorists think that fashion, like other designed forms, responds to the *Zeitgeist* theory, that is that fashion reflects the 'spirit of the age'. It is generally accepted that this is, at least partly, true so let us look at the various aspects of life in society which may influence the way we dress.

Politics

People who express an extreme or unusual political viewpoint often dress differently. Some do this because it is part of belonging to a group, others because they need to dress differently to stand out from the crowd. This is not a new concept. Politically inspired dress does not start and end with the freedom-fighter image of Che Guevara's camouflage-dressed and moustached comrades, or even with punks wearing 'Anarchy in the UK' T-shirts. People have been using dress to express political persuasion for many years. In seventeenth-century England, followers of King Charles I adopted a fancy and frilly style and were known as Royalists. Followers of Oliver Cromwell (an anti-Royalist and a republican) wore military-style dress and were known as Roundheads because of the helmet they wore as headgear. The Puritans, a religious Protestant group, who disapproved of the extravagant lifestyle of the Royalists, wore clothing which was dull, quite functional and very modest. All three of these groups, therefore, plainly demonstrated their political beliefs in their style of dressing. Even if not all the population of seventeenth-century England followed their styles precisely, they were still vastly influential in their time.

The law

The law of the land is not directly responsible for fashion styles any more, but if we go back to Salic law (a law for Salic Franks and other Germanic tribes) we can find many examples of the law governing what could and could not be worn. These are also known as sumptuary laws. Salic law, for example, forbade a woman to expose her forearm! There were obviously different moral and social reasons for these old sumptuary laws, and many of them were originally based on good old common sense. You only have to look today at the dress of religious orders who follow ancient or cultural dress codes which differ from contemporary styles, to see that they have many 'laws' relating to their style of dress which are now put down to custom or tradition but which originally may simply have been appropriate to the climate and their way of life.

The influence of law today is far more general; for example, even though laws have been introduced securing equality for women on many counts, it is still possible for some employers to frown on women who wear trousers. It was only after women got the right to vote that certain of them started wearing full-length trousers similar to men's. It is strange to think that it may take an act of parliament to radically alter styles of clothing!

Legal influences that may be more far-reaching in the future include European law, especially relating to trading within the European Community. The bringing-together of the EC has already exposed the European consumer to many new types of consumer products. Who knows how vast the impact of these laws will be! Only the consumer of the twenty-first century will really know the difference, as the influence of changes in the law can usually only be seen after a long time.

Marlene Dietrich, one of the most powerful role models in the 1930s advocating a mannish dress including trousers.

Technology

As many economies have become stronger through investment in manufacturing industries, and international trade barriers have been lowered, the demand for consumer goods has been met increasingly quickly and economic cycles have become shorter. This has been most evident in the twentieth century, with the enormous changes in technology which have taken place. We see the results daily in the seemingly never-ending stream of new products coming onto the market.

There are certain developments which have revolutionised the clothing industry. The invention of the washing machine and the introduction of relatively cheap synthetic fibres which are easy to care for have made it much easier for people to vary their style of dressing. This has increased the demand for new clothing enormously. The introduction of the sewing machine and, more recently, computers and lasers into garment production has enabled the industry to keep up with this increased demand. More interesting styles have become possible with the new fibres, most notably Lycra, introduced by the Dupont company. Leggings and swimming costumes, for example, would look very different without fibres like this which can stretch and mould themselves to the body. In fact, the development of clothing which is 'body conscious', in that it closely follows the contours of the body, would not have been possible at all without fibre technology.

The faster turnover of fashion clothing has resulted in styles being regenerated more quickly. Here are some striking examples of how key styles have quite obviously been repeated within this century.

The economy

The economy, mainly of the developed world, has a large part to play in influencing our attitude towards clothing and fashion. Some fashion historians, like James Laver, have attempted to link the ebb and flow of the economy's influence with the rise and fall of hemlines, that is when the economy is up so are hemlines, and when the economy is down so again are hemlines. This somewhat simplistic rule is difficult to apply when you look at the average high street today and see everything from the micro-mini to full-length skirts on women, and of course it does not apply to menswear at all! It is more useful to look at the overall effect of the economy on consumers.

Leisure shorts appeared with braces in the 1940s and reappeared as 'hot pants' in the 1970s; playsuits worn in the 1930s came back as baggy trousers in the 1980s.

The crisis silhouette: the dangerously revealing styles worn in late eighteenth-century France.

The post-crisis silhouette, epitomised by the flapper of the 1920s.

Laver has put forward what he calls the crisis and post-crisis theory, which states that at times of economic crisis the body form is emphasised and styles are ultra-feminine or ultra-masculine; when the economy improves the silhouette becomes looser and more relaxed. The illustrations on p. 12 back up this theory.

Individuals vary in their response to fluctuations in the economy. During a downturn, some people will cut down on their clothing budget. They will either 'play safe' and buy something plain, classic or functional or, contrarily, spend the last of the budget on a cheerful and extravagant item, to raise their morale. Let's face it, how many times have you bought something frivolous when times have been hard? It could have been a bar of chocolate or a ballgown – the effect would have been similar. When the economy is on the upturn, some people will spend, spend, spend on bright and exuberant clothes while others will try their hardest to look as though they don't need to spend money at all to achieve their style, by being either minimalist and simple or by wearing obviously low-status items. The 1960s is probably the best illustration of this, when some wore mini-skirts and vests while many wore second-hand clothes. Others even wore workmen's clothes like boiler suits, dungarees and donkey jackets. Status dressing can be turned on its head when the economy is good!

Assignments

1 Go to a museum with historical fashion collections (the Victoria and Albert Museum, Bath Museum of Costume, etc.) or look in a fashion history book. There are many to be found in libraries (see reference section). Pick a style from at least 30 years ago which you feel is being revived now in fashion stores. What similarities and differences are there between the original and the repeat? What influences are there that may or may not be in common? Make some sketches of both then and now which will illustrate your account. Use examples from womenswear, menswear and childrenswear if you can.

2 Do you agree that fashion is evolutionary? Find some examples of fashion today that you think can support your view.

3 Pick one example of each of the following:

   a) a trend
   b) a classic
   c) a fad

Find a photo or sketch (using fashion magazines) that best represents each style. Write about

   a) where it is now in its cycle
   b) where you think the style originated
   c) other influences on the style, e.g. media or status wearers

Then predict its future development.

Chapter 2

THE
DESIGNERS

Couture

When a couturier designs a collection of styles, they are made up and modelled for an invited audience. An individual can then have a particular style made up specially. This is rather like bespoke tailoring, where the clothes are 'made-to-measure'. The same style may be made up for other clients, too, but each one is made to fit the particular person. Each one is therefore unique. The price of these exclusive clothes is very high and this makes it unlikely that many people will be seen wearing them. However, most women do not like to discover that someone else has a dress just like theirs, especially when they have paid a lot for it. This is particularly so with celebrities, so some houses, especially in Paris, will refuse to make up a style a second time when an important client has already bought it.

How couture developed

In the nineteenth century, there were high-class dressmakers and court dressmakers for the upper classes and royalty. They made and copied clothing styles from Europe's rich and famous but they never really originated the styles. The most original clothes were theatrical in style, worn by flamboyant individuals who moved in aristocratic circles. Their dressmakers made clever use of the textile weavers' craft, by using Spitalfields silk or Lyons lace, or any other fabric highly valued for its beauty.

A British man from Yorkshire was to change all this. Charles Frederick Worth, who had some experience in the drapery field, and had worked in Paris, set up his own design and dressmaking establishment there in 1854. Worth turned the business on its head. Instead of copying what was the mood of the day by sending sketches with fabric swatches or samples to his clients, he produced a **collection** of made-up samples which were shown to customers, either individually or in small groups, on live models. This idea was dramatically new. Not only had he conceived the idea of the fashion show, but also he had mastered the art of selling a dream to women. The clients, whether young, old, fat or thin, could imagine themselves wearing the clothes and looking like the models – however unlikely that was in reality! Many other young couturiers followed in his footsteps, and also copied his example of selling to foreign trade buyers. Today, couture is still a thriving business, but not for quite the same reasons as in Worth's day. The licensing deals on related products and perfumes are now the main source of profit. (See p. 18.)

Paris couture organisation

The Chambre Syndicale de la Couture Parisienne (known in France as CSCP) was founded to represent the different sectors of the French fashion industry. Since 1975 it has had a ready-to-wear section to cater for the needs and protect the interests of designers in that sector. It now has an extended title: the Chambre Syndicale des Couturiers et des Créateurs de la Mode. Couturiers like to be distinguished from mere creators of fashion!

The CSCP is funded largely by the French government from a levy on all fashion-related goods and performs specific tasks on behalf of its members. Its main functions are to:

- coordinate dates of fashion shows in the spring and autumn seasons;
- issue press cards for the shows;
- regulate the release of photographs to the press;
- register all its members' new designs;
- regulate the conditions for copying;
- regulate the shipping of orders;
- represent its members in relations with the French government;
- regulate pay and conditions of service within that sector of employment;
- arbitrate in any dispute.

There is nothing much like it anywhere else in the world!

Couture shows are held twice a year, in early spring and early autumn. The designs are for those seasons so that customers can order, buy and wear the clothes almost immediately. The collections are shown to certain groups of people before others. First, they are shown to esteemed clients like Princess Diana, Paloma Picasso and Ivana Trump, and to the press. (The press often hold back on their reports if requested, to give other buyers a chance to release their versions.) Next, lower-ranking clients and trade buyers are invited to view. The trade buyers may buy a toile (a form of calico pattern or a copy of it), to take away and adapt for their own commercial purposes. Lastly, lower-ranking clients and students of fashion will be able to see the show. Today it is common for the press show to be put on video tape, and for this to be played to lower-ranking clients or students. If a client then wants to see a model in more detail, a house model (a woman employed to model for the couturier in the show) will wear it and model it for the client's inspection.

Couture in London, spring 1991.
A Norman Hartnell dress and robe (top right).
A Franka satin evening wrap (below).
A Victor Edelstein silk tweed suit (below right).

Additional sources of income

It is commonly acknowledged that the market for couture has dwindled, even if its influence has not. There are only about 5,000 women in the world who can afford couture so the dressmaking has become what is known as a **loss-leading** activity. This means that, although the designers gain a great deal of publicity and prestige, they actually lose money on their collections. Couturiers have to look for additional sources of income. These are some of the things that help them to make a profit.

Sales of related products

Perfume is first on this list. Others may be handbags, scarves, shoes, umbrellas and so on. Most of these are manufactured by licensees.

Licensing

A couturier may grant a licence to another company to produce goods under that couturier's name. The licence could include, amongst other things, use of the logo, or a distinguishing characteristic known as the **signature label**. For example, the signature label of Chanel handbags is the quilting. Christian Dior suits are another example of goods which may be made by a licensee. There is no limit to the number of licences that can be granted. Pierre Cardin alone has over 500 licensees and is now one of the most well-known designers in the world, as well as being one of the richest men alive.

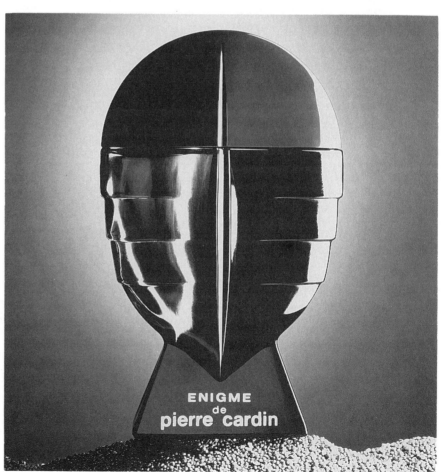

Licensed and related products like Pierre Cardin's perfume ranges create an image and back up the couture and ready-to-wear parts of the business.

Financial backing

Some houses are partly funded by large textile firms who will supply initial samples free and subsequently supply all that house's textile requirements. This type of arrangement often works extremely well.

Ready-to-wear

Most major couture houses design at least one ready-to-wear collection, as so few people buy from the couture collections. This will be discussed in depth later in this chapter.

Couture in other countries

Italy

Couture in Italy is based in Rome and organised, in a similar way to French couture, by the Camera Nazionale della Moda. Notable Italian couturiers are Valentino and Pucci.

USA

Couture here is not an organised set-up as in France and Italy, but nonetheless there are designers who will create exclusive designs for socially well-placed clients from, for example, the world of finance or government. Designers such as Halston and Oscar de la Renta are well known for dressing society's celebrities like Nancy Reagan and Ivana Trump.

United Kingdom

The couture scene here is also not organised, but there is a definite client base requiring tailored and refined designs for society or royal occasions. Their designers operate mainly from Mayfair addresses, and often set up near to, or in, Saville Row, famed for its men's bespoke tailoring. Some London couture designers are 'by appointment' to the Queen or Queen Mother, like Hardy Amies, or Hartnell. (The Hartnell house is now led by designer Marc Bohan, previously of Christian Dior in Paris.)

Ready-to-wear

While couture revolutionised the fashion scene in nineteenth-century France, ready-to-wear succeeded it as the major force in fashion after World War II. With much economic and social change after the war, the cost of couture could only be borne by a few, so couture designers and others began to change their approach rapidly. They started to produce ready-to-wear collections in addition to their main collections. Paris, New York, Milan and Tokyo have some of today's most influential designers' names on mass-produced high-fashion clothing. Such clothes have the leading edge in quality and can be clearly identified as coming from a particular house. Some ready-to-wear designers just have their own

PARIS
sehm
SALON INTERNATIONAL
DE L'HABILLEMENT MASCULIN
2.3.4.5
FEVRIER
1991
CARREFOUR MONDIAL
DE LA MODE MASCULINE
PARC DES EXPOSITIONS DE PARIS PORTE DE VERSAILLES PARIS XVe

An invitation to one of the world's largest menswear wholesale ready-to-wear fairs – SEHM in Paris.

exclusive outlets whilst others will sell their ranges to international wholesalers. Most do both. They will also sell related goods and license the use of their names on other product ranges.

The designer ready-to-wear shows are held twice a year in February/March and September/October in various locations. These are complemented by ready-to-wear exhibitions, some held at the same time, others held before or after the actual collections. These are for home rather than overseas buyers, who will wish to see the major trade shows at the same time as any designer 'catwalk' shows. All these shows preview designs for the following season, so they are about six months ahead of time. Table 1 shows the venues and trade show exhibitors in the major international centres.

The international arena for fashion in the ready-to-wear sector of the industry is now so well developed that even many small countries or those with limited exports get involved in fashion goods. Table 2 shows current developments in other centres outside the UK, highlighting trade shows and merchandise strengths within each country. It is not by any means a complete list.

Table 1   The international fashion arena   1: Major centres

Centre	Venues		Trade exhibitors
	Ready-to-wear designer collections	Trade shows	
Paris	Marquees in the Jardins des Tuileries or in the Cour Carée of the Louvre	Porte de Versailles	Première Vision – fabrics and textiles Salon du Prêt à Porter – women's ready-to-wear SEHM – men's ready-to-wear Salon de la Mode Enfantine – children's ready-to-wear
New York	In-house showrooms or various hired locations	Javits Convention Centre, Omni Park Centre, Seventh Avenue	New York Fabric Show – fabrics and textiles New York Pret – women's ready-to-wear Designer's Collective – men's ready-to-wear International Kids Show – children's ready-to-wear
Milan	In-house showrooms or various hired locations	Milan Fair (Campo Fiori Milano) Also a big venue on outskirts of Milan becoming popular	La Moda in Milano – women's ready to wear Many exhibitors of fashion, textiles and furnishings from the Milan area
London	Tents at Duke of York barracks in the Kings Road	Olympia	Fabrex – fabrics and textiles London Designer Show – women's ready-to-wear The London Show – young women's ready-to-wear Imbex – men and boys' ready-to-wear

An invitation to a designer ready-to-wear show in London.

Table 2 The international fashion arena 2: Other centres

Country/city	Trade shows/exhibitors	Specialities/strengths/drawbacks
Italy – Florence	*Pitti immagine bimbo* (childrenswear) *Pitti immagine uomo* (menswear) *Pitti immagine filati* (yarns etc.)	Good quality fashion at less than Milan prices.
Germany – Frankfurt – Cologne – Düsseldorf	*Interstoff* (fabrics) *Its Cologne* (womenswear) *Collections Premieren Düsseldorf* (womenswear and menswear) *Igedo* (womenswear)	Germany is Europe's largest clothing producer and produces some of the best-designed quality fashion garments in medium price ranges, such as *Escada, Mondi, Betty Barclay*. However, Germany has little foothold in the designer market.
Spain – Madrid – Barcelona	 *Gaudi Hombre* (menswear) *Gaudi Mujer* (womenswear)	Madrid houses a modest couture organisation – Alta Costura – which caters mainly for wealthy Spanish clients. A good source of moderately priced knitwear, leather and suede accessories, outerwear and shoes. Barcelona – fast becoming very trendy; home to newer breed of designers like Purificacion Garcia, Adolpho de Dominguez.
Portugal – Porto	*Portex* (menswear, womenswear and childrenswear)	Knitted garments.
Greece – Athens	*Unimode* (womenswear)	Dressy cocktail wear and sportswear. Prices often low, quality variable.
Denmark	Future Fashions Scandinavia Fair – attracts exhibitors from all over Scandinavia (menswear, womenswear and childrenswear)	Expensive, but with good styling features. Better-known labels: *In Wear, Matinique*.

Country/city	Trade shows/exhibitors	Specialities/strengths/drawbacks
Holland – Amsterdam	*Modam* (menswear and womenswear)	Style is casual; epitomised by their largest variety chain store, C&A.
Norway – Oslo	*Meteuken I Oslo* (fashion week)	Outerwear and sportswear particularly good.
Sweden – Stockholm	International Fashion Fair	Renowned for young contemporary styling of separates and outerwear. Labels include *Hennes* and *Mauritz*.
Ireland – Dublin	Futura Fair (fashion) Irish Craft, Gift and Fashion Fair	Notable designers: Pat Crowley, Paul Costelloe. High-quality craft production – tweeds and knits.
Japan		Everything from designerwear to jeans produced in high quality and large quantities. Garments produced for many European and American labels.
Hong Kong	Hong Kong Fashion Week	Now a high-quality producer, althoughy originally famous for trade in 'copied' styles (knock offs). When Hong Kong reverts to Chinese rule in 1997, there may be a decline (despite assurances from the government of China).
Taiwan, Korea, Singapore, The Philippines and Macau	Ispoasia (Singapore)	Cheaper cotton items a speciality. Produce many lines for export to Europe and America, often to buyer's specifications.
Turkey		A developing exporter of cotton tops, jeans and knitwear.
Israel		Sophisticated leatherwear, swimwear, sports and leisurewear. *Gottex* is a leading label.
India		Produces cheap textile products and is therefore a large exporter. Popular multiple store ranges like French Connection, Boules, Monsoon.
Romania, Poland, Yugoslavia, etc.		Craftwork, especially embroidered blouses. Small-scale production only; lacking modern technology.
Canada – Montreal	Canada International Womenswear Show	Thriving home market with obvious links to French styling and flair.
Brazil		Stylish swimwear, leisurewear; moderately priced shoes and other leather goods.
Argentina		Leather goods a speciality, including alligator skin.
Australia		Newest specialists in swimwear and leisurewear; strong ties to UK fashion scene. Ken Done is a leading designer, specialising in brightly coloured beachwear with abstract patterns.

Designer influences

The influence of designer-originated fashion on mainstream and mass-produced clothing is undeniable and many examples can be used to illustrate how a designer's idea can be exploited, without actually being copied directly. When David and Elizabeth Emanuel designed the wedding dress for Princess Diana, for her marriage to Prince Charles in 1981, it was a closely guarded secret until the great day. When the wedding was over, garment factories were buzzing with activity, each one intent on being the first to produce a 'copy'. Many 'copies' were available in West End and high street stores only 24 hours after the event. These companies were careful to copy the mood and style of the dress and not to infringe any copyright, although some companies have been known to blatantly ignore the law and to copy particularly successful styles or logo designs in order to increase sales. The process of blatant infringement of copyright law is known in the trade as 'knocking off'. 'Knock-offs' are sold in less salubrious surroundings than their designer originals. They are usually to be found in street markets or offered as 'off the back of a lorry'. Much copied merchandise consists of sports, leisure and luxury goods, for example Ralph Lauren 'Polo' shirts, the Lacoste 'crocodile' logo on sportswear and the Chanel crossed 'C' logo emblazoned on T-shirts or on jewellery.

Of course, not all designer influences are this obvious; most designer influences are more gradual and less easy to perceive. The best way to illustrate this is to look at current marketing theory on the subject.

The 'trickle down' theory or adoption process

This theory asserts that there is a sort of conspiracy amongst the fashion designers, the journalists and the elite clients to make a style become a fashion. This is how it works. The designers create a look or a particular style and introduce it in a fashion show. Whether the fashion press like the style or not depends heavily on the scale of their fashion show and the degree to which it is a success as both a social and a business event. Other elements such as outrageous outfits in the show which could merit the front page or a double-page spread, hospitality (for example champagne and comfortable surroundings for a press launch) and, more obviously, the degree of social contact with the designer and her/his clients, all help to interest the press. Friendly and press-hungry designers with famous and photogenic clients make for better news copy than designers who hold no fashion shows, shy away from interviews and who have little-known clients. You only have to look at the society pages in any issue of *Vogue*, *The Tatler*, and *Harpers and Queen* to see that many individual clients will secure good publicity for the designer they patronise. If those clients are from the Royal Family or from a particularly popular media or entertainment background, then the influence of that designer is more secure as many people will use the clients as role models and copy their style of dressing. Designers will, therefore, often offer garments or samples to specific personalities in order to acquire some free and prestigious advertising. That way they do each other a favour: one gets a free outfit and the other gets to influence his or her clients' friends and admirers. Many of us will deny aspiring to look like anyone else, yet we are all aware that it happens and that we may have copied 'a look', even if only from a friend or an acquaintance.

This then is the first stage of the trickle-down process. At the next stage, the style permeates each income group in turn.

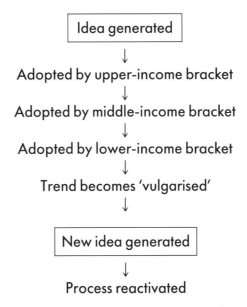

We can generally assume that those with the most money (regardless of class or social factors) will be the first to adopt a fresh idea, as it is usually more expensive when it is undiluted or **designer fashion** as it is called. Some of the cost factors are due to originality, and others to quality of production which is directly related, in most cases, to the originality factor. The style will then take months, or even years, to trickle down through the various income brackets until finally it appears in the bargain bins in high street stores, in seconds stores and on market stalls. Here it may be difficult to recognise because it will have been altered to make it cheaper to produce. The silhouette, fabric and details may all be somewhat different. When the style reaches this stage it has been vulgarised and will be ridiculed by those who wore it a few months, or perhaps years, earlier. (The version they wore will, of course, have been of better quality.) Needless to say, style leaders will have dropped the style by then and moved on to something new. Think how often, even among friends, you have heard someone say: 'Oh no! Look what she's wearing! They went out *ages* ago.' It is perhaps unfortunate that being in fashion or not is regarded by many as a measure of a person's social success. Those whose clothes are unfashionable are often looked down on as socially inept.

The garments which are discarded at the end of the trickle-down process are usually not worn out in any way whatsoever as it is mainly social acceptability which spurs people on to buy new clothes. Many of these discarded fashions then trickle down further by being resold as second-hand goods in charity shops such as Oxfam or in jumble sales.

Copyright and design protection

Copyright is the right of a creator, whether a designer of clothes or the author of a book, to indicate that their work is their own 'intellectual property'. This means that it was originated by them and they lay claim to the idea by registering copyright, that is a right to their original copy. Subsequently, anyone wishing to copy their idea should ask permission and, in most cases, pay a fee for the privilege of using it. Songwriters, for example, usually charge a fee each time one of their songs is used commercially. Most fashion designers, on the other hand, prefer not to allow any copying. If copies are made without permission, copyright is said to have been 'infringed'.

Pucci prints have been much copied over the years (original below, copy right).

The simplest form of design protection is a form of copyright claimed by signing and dating the designers' original drawings. Because it can be expensive for a designer to pursue a claim against another designer or manufacturer for copying, claims are not always taken to court, and a lot are actually settled out of court. So it is almost impossible to prevent original designs from being copied, but copiers can be severely penalised if the claim is successfully upheld in court. Penalties may include confiscation of the goods and liability for damages towards the injured party. The most recent legislation is the Copyright Design and Patents Act 1988 (known as CDPA).

With graphic work such as a fashion design, the designs are protected 'irrespective of artistic quality', and they must be 'original'. The designer is the copyright owner unless the designer is working for a company, when the company owns the copyright. The copyright then lasts for the designer's life plus 50 years. It is important to note that only the *drawings* of the design hold the copyright and not the finished article. Most infringements of copyright occur when copiers make copies with style or detail alterations. Small alterations do not free the copier from infringement because a direct link with the original work can be observed. There are, however, various sources of help and advice on this matter:

Registrar Stationers Company
Stationers Hall
London EC4M 7BB
Tel. 071-248-2934

Design Protection Advisory Service
The Design Council
28 Haymarket
London SW17 4SU
Tel. 071-839-8000

Patent Office
25 Southampton Buildings
Chancery Lane
London WC2A 1AX
Tel. 071-831-2525

The original design drawing should be marked © with the year of design and the name of the designer. A copy can then be deposited with the Stationers Hall Registrar; or alternatively with a bank manager or solicitor in exchange for a dated receipt.

Design registration, which is a stronger protection than copyright, can be done at the Patent Office. A design can be registered as a patent if, for instance, it contains significantly innovative manufacturing processes, but patents are mainly for inventions, mechanisms and systems.

Assignments

1 *Designer report*

Using back copies of consumer magazines and newspapers find an example of an American, a French, an Italian and a British designer.

a) For each one, describe their style and design specialities

b) Describe which of their styles have influenced retail/ mainstream fashion recently, giving examples of which retail ranges you think illustrate this.

Illustrate your report using cuttings from magazines and newspapers, and by making sketches of garments available at retailers.

2 *Trends analysis*

Write a report, summarising the main trends from designer collections for this season. Use the following headings:

a) Colours and fabrics

b) Themes

c) Silhouettes

d) Styles and garments

e) Details, trims and accessories

Give at least one designer example for each trend which you identify under the headings. Illustrate your report using magazine and newspaper cuttings or your own sketches.

3 *Designer profile*

Write a historical and factual profile of a favourite designer of your choice (couture or ready-to-wear). Consider how they entered their chosen profession, what training they had, how long they have been in business, their successes (and failures!), awards and accolades.

Use your local or college library or historical sources. If the designer is current their public relations firm may offer help.

Chapter 3

THE
STREET

The birth of the teenager and youth culture

The term 'teenager' was coined by the American advertising agency J. Walter Thompson, to describe adolescents in the early 1950s. Never before had there been so many who had it so good. Let's examine some of the reasons that led J. Walter Thompson to identify teenagers as a specific consumer group.

Post-war baby-boom

In post-war Britain the government introduced the Welfare State, which provided security for young families through income supplements like unemployment benefits and family allowances, and through state housing provision. These policies helped in encouraging a sharp rise in the birth-rate, so that in the late 1950s the proportion of teenagers in the population began to increase significantly. This trend continued into the 1980s. (At present the teenage population is declining but it is expected to start rising again from 1995.)

Changes in the education system

The 1944 Education Act made it compulsory for young people to stay on at school until the age of 15 – the school leaving age was subsequently raised to 16 in the early 1970s. Previously, young people had been able to leave school and start work at 14 years of age. These changes lifted a great deal of responsibility from young people in terms of wage earning and other adult responsibilities. Increased state provision of further and higher education meant that more young people, regardless of class, could in theory enter colleges and universities on merit. From the 1960s on, going to college was normal for many young people who would never have experienced it if they had been born fifty years earlier.

The media

Media coverage and international communications developed rapidly after World War II and this led people to seek knowledge and to aspire to new lifestyles. American TV programmes and products brought new concepts into British homes, so people inevitably desired the products and accepted the values of the fast-developing consumer culture. As the post-war economy improved, so did the living standards of all age groups and some people claimed class distinctions became less important. Music styles imported from the USA on radio and gramophone records led to the growth of 'popular' music, now known as 'pop', a phenomenon as varied as its roots, which lay in rhythm and blues and rock and roll.

Combine these background influences with a growing teenage population and there you have it: **youth culture**, a post-war phenomenon. Here was an enormous new market, eager for constant change and stimulation.

Youth sub-cultures

The term 'dominant culture' in a sociological sense refers to the ways in which the majority of people think and act in society as a result of social interaction rather than genetic inheritance. Sub-cultures are smaller cultures co-existing within the common culture and may be grouped according to:

social class
ethnic origin
religion
politics
age

Some of these categories are more conscious of how society sees them than others; youth sub-cultures are definitely aware of their impact.

Some youth groups are sub-cultural because their style of dress and behaviour is in opposition to mass culture and because they have different values and live by anti-social rules. Most sub-cultural youth groups dress to shock or to provoke comment, and seek to set themselves apart from the crowd. Even in an early youth-cult film like *The Wild One* with Marlon Brando, the hero is an outsider who dresses differently and acts in such a way as to alienate himself from the adults portrayed in the film. Equivalent female heroines of such ilk were not really evident until Marianne Faithfull in *Girl on a Motorcycle* and later Toyah Wilcox in *Jubilee*. The 'young rebel' is now a constant image reinforced in everything from advertisements to television soap operas.

There are some general features which may help to characterise different youth sub-cultures:

strong group identity   This is often reflected in uniformity of dress.
desire for self-expression   They frequently make a stand against society's values; for example, hippies with their communal lifestyle.
individuality   They like to be different from all other groups.

Marlon Brando, one of the original leather-jacketed rebels in the 1950s film The Wild One.

sense of territory   They frequent certain places and discourage others from being there; for example, punks in subways in London.

creativity   Many of their clothes and hairstyles are original and interesting.

Some groups have values which reflect anti-social or deviant trends. These fall into several categories.

counter-culture   This favours alternative or negative values such as those expressed in songs like 'Anarchy in the UK', recorded by The Sex Pistols in the late 1970s. The punk style of dressing also reflects anti-establishment values.

retreat   This goes further than counter-culture in adopting an alternative lifestyle; for example, living in communes and practising natural farming methods, like some of the early hippies.

radical   This involves extreme political or religious aims. Since the late 1960s skinheads were linked with the British National Party and the National Front, both groups advocating violence and racism.

conformity   This trend is to conform to a strict code of dress or lifestyle, with the aim of being socially acceptable. The Sloanes exemplified this in the late 1970s, with their very 'proper' style of dress.

All these groups and trends have had an impact on the commercial fashion scene.

Street fashion

Youth sub-cultural style is now a constant part of the fashion scene and is known popularly as street fashion. It has influenced mainstream fashion today as much as any designer creations. Street fashions come and go, and some may appear to defy definition, but here is a short guide to street-fashion spotting.

Acid house

Closely related to the music which rocketed to popularity in clubs from 1987, the style is loosely based on hippy clothing in the 1970s and the psychedelic era. It was characterised by loose sweatshirts, 'smiley' logos, baggy joggers, bright and acid colours, bandanas, headbands and ponchos.

'B' boys

Famed for break-dancing, a mid-1980s' dance craze that involved lots of spinning and robotic movements to electro or hip-hop music. Because they often spun on their heads, baseball caps were essential and were combined with satin bomber jackets, trainers and baggy jeans or joggers. 'B' boys are referred to collectively as 'crew'.

Beatniks

Juliet Greco, the idol of beatnik girls, wore long black hair, a fringe, black eyeliner, black capri pants and a black polo-neck sweater. Beatniks popularised jazz clubbing and the Parisienne habit of sitting in cafés like those in Saint-Germain. Coffee bars sprang up in London's Soho to accommodate the young 'bon vivants' so aptly described in novels such as Colin MacInnes's *Absolute Beginners*, which was made into a film in the mid-1980s.

Bikers

Derived from Hell's Angels, this is a cult group originally of American biking fanatics with distasteful personal habits. The biker, however, also wears the colour of dissension – black – with the material of rebellion – leather – mixed with a touch of dirty denim. The biker listens to heavy metal music bands like Iron Maiden and praises all that is macho – even female bikers do this!

Casuals

Casuals ruled the soccer terraces of the 1980s in Fila tracksuits, Nike trainers, wedge hairstyles and Lacoste polo shirts. Their effect has been wide-ranging; like earlier mods with 'Fred Perry' shirts, they brought label consciousness to the working classes, and sharp hairstyles into vogue, the wedge and flickbacks being of great overall influence.

Fly girls and homeboys

This is a natural progression from the American ragamuffin style, which is a parody on street urchins for young blacks. With exaggerated cap-style headgear, the fly girl and homeboy listen to hip-hop and any type of rare groove funk. Their casual clothing is so over-sized that it swamps some youngsters who tuck their huge jogger bottoms into quality socks and 'Timberland' boots or high-top trainers, left casually undone with the tongue hanging over the laces. They popularised the use of bum bags, money pouches, hooded sweatshirts, baseball caps and so on in a bright mixture of casual style. They also borrowed items from the Rasta repertoire, for example African pendants and batik print shirts.

Hippies

Rebel *with* a cause, the hippy went back to nature, wore long hair and bohemian-style clothing, and adopted a 'love not war' stance, vegetarianism and vaguely left-wing politics, among many other things. Ethnic, handmade or second-hand clothing was most popular with the original and now the modern hippy. Many members of this sub-culture have been hippies since the 1970s or earlier; others are recent converts.

Mods and rockers

The film *Quadrophenia* with The Who and their music attempted to portray all that mods and rockers stood for. 'Modernists', as they were originally called, wore sharply styled imported Italian suits, later to be topped off with Parka jackets. 'Modettes' (mod girls) wore 1960s minimalist style, op-art mini shift dresses and well-cut bobs. The essential item was an Italian scooter – Lambretta or Vespa adorned with chrome mirrors and nicknacks. Their archrivals, the rockers, wore biker clothing, listened to rock 'n' roll and rode 'real' bikes. The bikes and the clothing were what they argued and fought about so vehemently. Mod style has been revived many times since its introduction but usually without the bikes and the music.

New romantics

A street style of the early 1980s which mimicked the Victorian romantics in style and was popularised by the 'pirate' collection of Vivienne Westwood in 1981–2 and bands such as Spandau Ballet and Adam and the Ants. The look was all velvet and frills and also became known as the 'Princess Di' look as she wore versions of it. Incorporating dreadlocks into the look became very popular in the wake of Boy George and 'white Rasta' bands like Hayzi Fantayzi, so the look started off with made-up romantic decadence and ended with mock ethnic exoticism.

Punks

The prime example of street style, punk was first noticed in 1976 in London art schools. Punks enshrined negative values, and worked very hard at being against fashion and consumerism. Punk was famous for black plastic bin-liners, safety pins, bondage straps and zips. Punk has had many guises since 1976 but punks can still be seen in cities across the UK, whether they stick to the original styles or have broadened into styles like 'gothic', which is a cross between new romantic and punk, or 'psychobilly', which blends punk with rockabilly styling (see Teddy boys).

Rastas

Rastafarianism is strictly speaking a religion and culture, but a lot of young people follow some of the ways of rasta because they like the look or the values, or both. Rastas dress in the 'roots' style with African fabrics and accessories such as the huge knitted caps which encompass their 'locks' (hair which has developed into matted 'dreadlocks' by being left natural or matted). Rastas also smoke ganja (marijuana) to achieve a spiritual 'high', and listen to reggae music by bands like Bob Marley and the Wailers and I Roy.

Skinheads

Although the early skinheads listened to 'ska' and reggae music, both black music styles, the popular received interpretation of skinhead is that of Fascist, racist, violent young working-class people often associated with the National Front. The skinhead style embodies an element of urban storm trooper with its closely cropped heads, stomping Doc Marten boots, and army surplus jackets over workaday jeans.

Teddy boys

One of the earliest street-style movements, also known as Teds, the style consisted of a drape jacket with a dress shirt and bootlace tie. It parodied Edwardian gentlemen's dressing, hence the name 'Teddy boy'. The sharply dressed young men wore their hair tight at the neck and loosely coiffed and greased into a shape known as a DA or duck's arse, after the effect that it gave at the back of the head. The effect of Teddy boys on the British public was that of indignant outrage. They loved and made popular rock-and-roll music, played then by Bill Haley and the Comets and Elvis Presley. More contemporary revivals of the Ted style have included rockabilly, which shares music and hair styles. It is a little more casual and folksy with check shirts and western-style jeans but retains the bootlace tie detail.

Influence of street fashion

Street fashion, by the same token as designer fashion, influences the mainstream but in a unique way. Where designer fashion starts with the wealthy individual, street fashion starts with those who have more innovative courage than hard cash. Again, let us take a look at a marketing theory to get an idea of how the process works.

The 'trickle-across' theory

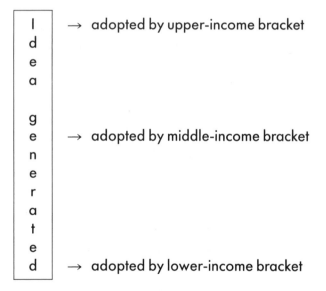

The idea may be adopted by all income groups simultaneously in the trickle-across theory. It is based on the idea that if a group of people with little influence in other realms can inject interest into their style of dress, then that style may be adopted by people in other groups. The theory certainly holds true with street fashion. When a style which has similar features to those worn by a particular young group is put on the market, it is often popular, especially with those in the same age group as the originators of the style. Awareness of this tendency can help those in the fashion industry to predict the likely success (or otherwise) of certain styles.

There are different versions of the trickle-across theory but the basic idea remains the same: that young, classless individuals have the power to influence others. Some of the best examples of this in action have been the most dramatic: new romantics influencing Princess Diana's style of romantic dress; punk style remodelled as 'punkature', a collection by Zandra Rhodes which made punk most glamorous.

The trickling-across of punk meant that lots of young men and women wore black zip-up tops with ornamental zip pockets, bondage style straps on their ankle boots and studs on their jeans. The men even wore two or more earrings without much risk of losing their jobs, because parts of punk style, by trickling across, came to be included in the mainstream fashion styling of the day and even reappeared in other designer collections, perpetuating its stylistic influence. Whatever happens, when mainstream fashion picks up on an idea which has started as a street fashion, then the originators either change their style completely or become more extreme, so gradually the original style loses popularity and eventually becomes extinct.

Trickling-across will continue to happen as long as there are young people around to start the ball rolling by dressing differently.

Stripey ribs and jersey items became a popular street trend in the early 1990s – to be trickled across into retail outlets very shortly afterwards. The illustrations show street fashion (below) and retail fashion (right).

Chapter 4

THE
PRODUCERS

The creation of a style

Fashion industry designers for the mass-produced or retail sector work in a similar way to the ready-to-wear designers, but their source of ideas may be different. They have tighter cost restraints, so that we, the consumers, can actually afford to buy what they produce, while the end product is acceptable to us in terms of quality and style. The conceptual stages of creating a range of high-street fashion merchandise are quite far removed from the glossy image we have of designers at work in their studios. The popular phrase in the trade is that a good range is '1 per cent inspiration, 99 per cent perspiration'! Let us look more closely at the process.

Stage 1: Inspiration

A designer, or group of designers, will look at various sources to get strong ideas for styles which will appeal to their company's target market. Where they look depends on what motivates their customers.

The media

They play an important role in communicating trends to both trade and public. Magazines are first to report on designer clothes. A designer may look at a trade magazine report on womenswear for the following year, and then may incorporate some of the features into a range, even if they are only small features such as the line of the collar, or fold of the cut. International fashion magazines are very popular as they can bring very many different interpretations of fashion and style to bear. Good examples would be the entire *International Vogue* range, or *Womenswear Daily*, a New York fashion-oriented paper. The home market, of course, will have its own specialities, so designers for teenage retail fashion outlets will just as readily scan *Smash Hits* as they will *DR The Fashion Business*.

Designers also keep a close eye on major trends emerging from television, films and music. Can you imagine what teenager has not heard of Kylie Minogue or Madonna but, more to the point, how many of them emulate them in style of dress? Big screen films also have a massive influence: Meryl Streep in *Out of Africa* started a trend for colonially inspired fashions in softer colours and fabrics. These styles are just some that have really made an impact in the high street.

Fashion prediction consultancies

Since the 1970s there has been a massive growth in this area of business. Companies range from designer consultant specialist firms who produce colour palettes, style ideas and market reports at least one season in advance, to companies who specialise in colour and fabrics and will issue forecasts at least eighteen months in advance of the retail season. (See also Chapter 7.)

Trade shows

Designers will also visit trade shows, especially fabric fairs like Fabrex in England, Interstoff in Germany and Première Vision in France. The ideas from these shows will be more general than dramatic but will point the designer in a practical direction. (See also Chapter 2.)

Stage 2: Design

This is a surprisingly quick process during which quick yet technically accurate sketches are drawn so that a working pattern can be devised. At this stage fabric swatches are selected. These are small fabric samples in different colours and prints.

A major consideration in design is the time of year when the garment will be sold, that is what season it is to be marketed for.

Autumn

This is Britain's longest season in terms of fashion. Samples for this season are shown to the retail trade mainly in February and March.

Christmas/cocktail

This is a short season where all the designs are given a dressy interpretation. Some firms, however, specialise in this type of merchandise all the year round with various seasonal inspirations.

Cruise/resort

This is the season for high-class casual and holiday outfits. It is a short season in the UK for most customers. However, for the top end of the market it is first retailed in December and January, and trade is brisk right around the year. Trendsetters in this market look to St Tropez and other 'jetset' holiday locations for their inspiration.

Spring

For this, Britain's second-longest season, samples are shown to the retail trade mainly in September and October.

Summer

This season is almost non-existent here due to the climate. The cruise/resort collections tend to cater for most holiday styles whereas in places like Rio de Janeiro in Brazil summer daywear is a top seller. Men's shorts, for example, sell there as formal businesswear in that season! Most British retailers use this season to trial style or colour ideas for the autumn season or to launch 'back to school' styles for junior retail outlets.

The first collection of sketches, which is instigated by the buyer, selector, or in-house design director, will be pared down to form a commercially viable line and variations on these will be drawn. The buyer, selector or design director will select certain designs to be samples.

Stage 3: First samples

Sample lengths of fabric and quantities of the other materials needed are ordered. These include interlining, lining, fusibles, wadding, shoulder pads, buttons, zips and belts. Sample patterns are then cut by the designer or an assistant so as to closely resemble the sketch. This and the component materials are cut out and passed to a sample machinist for make-up. The sample machinists are highly skilled. They can work through all aspects of a garment's production and make valuable suggestions to a designer or pattern cutter if they feel that a sample could be made in a better or more cost-effective way. It is at this stage that a costing (wholesale) can be prepared, when all the practical elements are complete. This gives a guide as to price until the factory can finally set a firm price.

Stage 4: Sample showing

The samples, and sometimes the whole range, are shown to the buyer, selector or design director plus any supporting team required. Small fashion shows may be staged in-house. Designs and samples are analysed, methods of manufacture are considered and costings are discussed. It is at this stage that some samples are firmly rejected, often to be sold at warehouse sample sales. This does not mean that the garment is imperfect but is often that it is considered too expensive and too difficult to mass produce, or even too advanced or too dull in terms of style.

Stage 5: Redesign

Any alterations or modifications required are incorporated into new samples, and the process is repeated from Stage 2 onwards until the finished sample is considered perfect.

Stage 6: Orders placed

First orders can be placed one year in advance especially by variety chains such as Marks & Spencer, who buy from manufacturers on a large scale and are not so much affected by minor style changes or fads. The majority of fashion retailers place bulk orders at trade shows or in wholesale showrooms, one season (about six months) in advance of trading, and from then on can be buying and placing orders at any time, up to and including the trading period. Fast-moving fashion retailers catering for the junior market will need this flexibility to respond to fads or other fashion quirks without delay. The period between order and delivery can sometimes be as short as ten weeks. Orders are often placed in units of one dozen pieces, or in size packs of, for example, five pieces: two size 10s, two size 12s and one size 14.

Stage 7: Sealing samples

A sealing sample range is a range of garments produced by the manufacturer. It is at this stage that the final garment quality is best assessed. Retailers will ask the manufacturer to submit a sealing sample with the following:

> a complete size chart
> a technical specification chart
> a sketch of the garment with a fabric swatch

The sample is then passed to the designer and either to an in-house sample technologist or to the buyer or selector, so that the quality can be assessed in relation to the original sample. The specification can also be checked for accuracy. For example, they may check whether the fabric washes well with the recommended wash/care instructions.

Some fashion companies are reluctant to provide any sealing samples, as the original sample is usually very impressive and some outworkers will produce work of a variable nature. As fashion retailers demand better-quality clothing for their customers, the fashion companies will be coming under greater pressure to produce sealing sample ranges. Some of the variety chains or multiples require a sealing sample range to be produced in all sizes to be sold. This is to ensure that the same quality is evident in a small size as in an extra large.

Stages 1 to 7 make up what is known as the **conceptual** or **sampling process**.

The production

Once the sample has been passed or sealed, it is taken from the hands of the designer and the production of the garment is carried out by a separate factory, sometimes known as an outworker. This process is also called **CMT** or cut, make and trim, as this is all they do.

Pattern making

Outworkers often make their own production patterns based on the sample pattern. These can be originated in two dimensions (known as cutting on the flat) from a flat block, which is a type of blueprint template. Patterns can also be made from toile, a type of calico, which is draped on a tailor's dummy. This three-dimensional method is often used for unusual details, close-fitting garments or drapes and folds. The toile is later transferred to a paper pattern for commercial use.

Grading

The sample size is often a midway size in the range, such as size 12. A grader will produce identical patterns for the different sizes in the range by using mathematical gradients or ratios which relate to current sizing standards. So a pattern can be graded up to sizes 14, 16, 18 and so on or graded down to sizes 10 and 8.

A women's block bikini in nine sizes produced by a computer grading program. This was done on an Assyst flat-bed plotter.

This grading can be done by hand and is a highly skilled job requiring years of training and experience. A computer can do the same task in a matter of minutes. It tends to be the larger firms that use this faster method, as a computer grader is a major capital expense, but some clothing industry centres, like training centres, colleges and so on, will hire them out to clothing businesses.

BIKINI BLOCK

SIZES 34 36 38 40 42 44 46 48 50

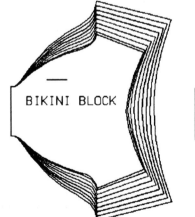

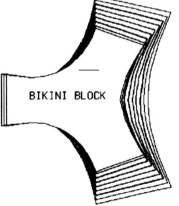

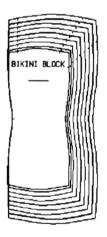

Sizing

There is an international organisation for standardisation known as the ISO, which is attempting to standardise all measurements and sizes. Metrication and membership of the EC have helped British people to begin to understand comparative sizes, if not comparative sizing methods. There is still a lot of debate as to whether an international set of standards is needed, if indeed possible. National or regional figure types, which result from varying standards of living and specific diets, are the main reasons for this. The British Standards Institute, meanwhile, have produced their own recommendations based on the Swedish Centilong System (1958), which uses height as an invariable basis for regimented clothing. The only variable is therefore girth, so a size 12 denotes an average height with a range of sizes for particular measuring points such as bust, waist, and shoulder to wrist. The main exceptions to this system are large, tall, and petite ranges for clothing, which often have varying lengths available. This is particularly true of menswear retail, where it is standard practice to stock, for example, more than one length of trouser in trouser ranges. Infants' and children's clothing is also an exception in that length or height is now being used more than age group as a guide to size. These two methods are often used in conjunction, e.g. 80 centimetres / 12 months.

The lay

Once the pattern is complete it has to be laid onto the fabric for cutting – a stage known as **the lay**. The lay is first estimated by placing scale pieces onto graph paper. This is also a highly skilled task as the lay should utilise maximum space on the fabric with minimum waste. The **lay plan** will also mark where pattern notches occur and will match stripes, checks, patterns and one-way naps. Of course this task is now vastly simplified by the use of computer lay programs, which plan the optimum use of space in the minimum time. The hardware for this task, which includes plotter equipment, is very costly, and is still mainly used only by the larger garment producers in this country.

An example of a computer lay-planning printout for precision-marking the lay to be specified to the CMT factory. This was done by an Assyst automatic layplanner.

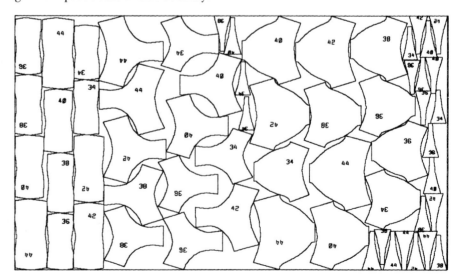

A technical size and specification chart giving typical women's body measurements for combined height and girth covering a wide range of dimensions. This type of size chart would be used by pattern and grading technicians.

Body measurements for medium bust development:
Increments are based on an increase of 5 cm girth and 2.4 cm height

Area		10	12	14	16	18	20	22	Increment
1	Height	159.6	162.0	164.4	166.8	169.2	171.6	173.0	2.4
2	Weight (Pounds)	102	118	134	150	166	182	198	16lb
3	Hip	87.0	92.0	97.0	102.0	107.0	112.0	117.0	5.0
4	Bust	81.0	86.0	91.0	96.0	101.0	106.0	111.0	5.0
5	Waist	61.0	66.0	71.0	76.0	81.0	86.0	91.0	5.0
6	Chest	77.4	81.0	84.6	88.2	91.8	95.4	99.0	3.6
7	Top hip (11.0 cm from waist)	81.0	86.0	91.0	96.0	101.0	106.0	111.0	5.0
8	Ribcage (under bust)	66.0	71.0	76.0	81.0	86.0	91.0	96.0	5.0
9	Neck	35.0	36.0	37.0	38.0	39.0	40.0	41.0	1.0
10	Bicep	24.7	26.5	28.3	30.1	31.9	33.7	35.7	1.8
11	Elbow	23.7	25.5	27.3	29.1	30.9	32.7	34.5	1.8
12	Wrist	15.2	16.0	16.8	17.6	18.4	19.2	20.0	0.8
13	Thigh	49.8	53.0	56.2	59.4	62.6	65.8	69.0	3.2
14	Knee	32.6	34.0	35.4	36.8	38.2	39.6	41.0	1.4
15	Calf	31.6	33.0	34.4	35.8	37.2	38.6	40.0	1.4
16	Ankle	22.3	23.0	23.7	24.4	25.1	25.8	26.5	0.7
17	X-chest	29.8	31.0	32.2	33.4	34.6	35.8	37.0	1.2
18	X-back (12cm down from nape)	31.8	33.0	34.2	35.6	36.8	38.0	39.2	1.2
19	Shoulder length	11.7	11.9	12.1	12.3	12.5	12.7	12.9	0.2
20	Scye width	10.1	11.0	11.9	12.8	13.7	14.6	15.5	0.9
21	Scye depth	17.5	18.1	18.7	19.3	19.9	20.5	21.1	0.6
22	Bust width	17.8	19.0	20.2	21.4	22.6	23.8	25.0	1.2
23	Nape to bust	32.6	34.0	35.4	36.8	38.2	39.6	40.0	1.4
24	Nape to waist over bust	51.8	53.0	54.2	55.6	56.8	58.0	59.2	1.2
25	Nape to waist centre back	40.4	41.0	41.6	42.2	42.8	43.4	44.0	0.6
26	Nape to hip	62.1	63.0	63.9	64.8	65.7	66.6	67.5	0.9
27	Nape to knee	97.5	99.0	100.5	102.0	103.5	105.0	106.5	1.5
28	Nape to floor	137.9	140.0	142.1	144.2	146.3	148.4	150.5	2.1
29	Sleeve length (outer)	57.1	58.0	58.9	59.8	60.7	61.6	62.5	0.9
30	Sleeve length (inner)	43.1	43.5	43.9	44.3	44.7	45.1	45.5	0.4
31	Abdominal seat diameter	21.3	23.0	24.7	26.4	28.1	29.8	31.5	1.7
32	Hip width	30.2	31.8	33.4	35.0	36.6	38.2	39.8	1.6
33	Body rise	27.9	29.0	30.1	31.2	32.3	33.4	34.5	1.1
34	Shoulder angle (degrees)	20.5	20.5	20.5	20.5	20.5	20.5	20.5	NIL
35	Outside leg	100.5	102.0	103.5	105.0	106.5	108.0	109.5	1.5

Conversion from metric to imperial

0.3 cm = ⅛ in
0.6 cm = ¼ in
0.9 cm = ⅜ in
1.2 cm = ½ in
1.5 cm = ⅝ in
1.8 cm = ¾ in
2.1 cm = ⅞ in
2.5 cm = 1 in

Source: Patrick Taylor, *Computers in the Fashion Industry*, Heinemann, 1990, p.62.

A lay on the cutting table after the bulk of the cutting has been completed.

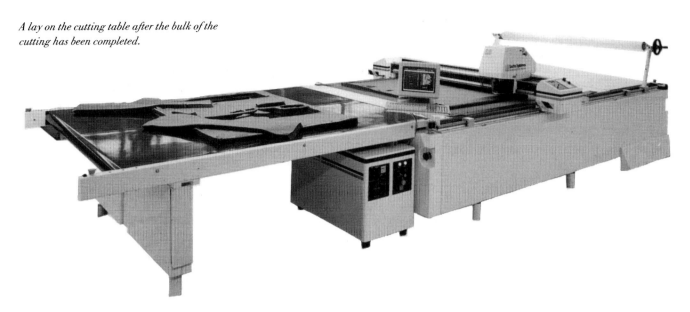

Laying and cutting

A bolt, or roll, of fabric is then automatically unrolled and placed, layer upon layer, onto a large cutting table by a roll conveyor. The garment pieces are cut either manually with a band knife, which is almost like a jigsaw, or by computer-programmed, vibration-free cutting heads. The most advanced factories can now use laser cutting methods, programmed by the lay computer. Volume producers, like jeans manufacturers, who use one shape very often, sometimes use cast metal dies. These cut large quantities of fabric in the same way that a pastry cutter cuts through soft pastry to make shapes.

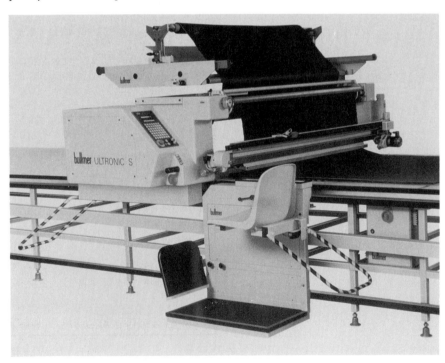

A laying-up machine with capacity for extra fabric roll storage.

Batching and piece-work

The garment pieces, when cut, are batched and arranged in the order in which they will be sewn. The garments are then made up in the factory by machinists who are piece-workers, that is they are paid according to what they produce. Each machinist carries out a particular task, such as stitching side seams, top-stitching collars or attaching pockets. These tasks are often rotated amongst the machinists to avoid boredom and maintain productivity levels.

There are many faults which can occur during manufacture. These are just some of them:

Stitching or overlocking comes undone.

Buttons or trims fall off.

Padding/wadding/interlining either loses its shape or becomes detached.

Seams open.

Seams pucker.

Seams are unmatched.

Patterns (checks, stripes, etc.) are unmatched.

Trim (braiding, pocket, etc.) is uneven or crooked.

Each task may be timed and then costed to give a price element to each stage of production. Time and productivity management is a constant source of debate in the clothing industry today. However, most CMT manufacturers still have their perks: 'cabbage', a familiar term in the fashion trade, is a garment (or van load of garments!) made from leftover material which is of no use to the client. Sometimes 'cabbage' can be contrived by 'squeezing' the lay. However it is achieved, it is sold at a near clear profit for the CMT manufacturer. Any pieces of cloth which are too small for 'cabbage' are bundled into bags and sold as 'fents'. These are often recycled and made into felting for soundproofing or carpet underlay, amongst other things. There is very little waste in the garment trade!

Finishing and despatching

The final touches are applied to the garments as they near the end of the production line. Any buttons or button-holes are completed and the garment is finally pressed, mainly by huge steam-powered irons at ironing benches with vacuum blow tables, or by a Hoffman presser. Very automated factories use a type of steam injection method where garments are rapidly passed over a perforated mannequin, which is similar to the garment shape, and steam is shot through the perforations to provide a crease-free garment. These garments are then either bagged flat or hung with garment bags over the hangers, ready for despatch in specially designed garment vans or lorries. These have built-in garment racks so the garments are delivered in the same condition as they will be stored and eventually sold. This saves an enormous amount of time at the fashion retail outlets.

The mediation

Checking on garment quality is a task performed at many stages of sampling and production, yet the buying team of a fashion retail outlet will need to satisfy themselves that quality checking is maintained to their own high standards. Larger retail outlets, such as department store chains, variety chains and multiples, will have their own teams of textile and garment technologists. Small retail outlets, especially independents, will rely almost totally on the product knowledge of the buyer, or, if in doubt, will ask an independent quality control laboratory for an assessment.

The costing

There are two agreed methods of costing, the first being just as workable as the second.

Method A

Think of a price.
Double it.
Add VAT.
This method requires years of experience in the garment trade. The acid test is whether the buyer will buy at this price and then whether the manufacturer goes bankrupt at the end of a season! If in doubt about bankruptcy see the back pages of *DR The Fashion Business* and count the number of firms that are either bankrupt or are undergoing some form of legal winding-up process. As *DR The Fashion Business* is a weekly publication, you can see that the turnover of small manufacturers is rapid.

Method B

This is based on the premise that there is an average of between ten and forty operations per garment and an average throughput time (from cut to trim) of one to three weeks. Add together the following:

> number of components in the garment $\times$ £X
> number of standard operations $\times$ £Y
> number of non-standard operations $\times$ £Z

This should equal labour costs plus the cost of all materials plus fixed order costs at £A per unit (administration, planning, etc.) plus overheads at £B per unit (lighting, power, etc.) plus percentage profit margin plus VAT. This then gives a wholesale or cost price. To calculate the retail or selling price a retailer will add the retail per cent profit margin.

An example of a costing sheet showing precise costs for each operation, and for related items and activities.

COSTING SHEET

CONTRACT DESCRIPTION

Check party dress

Reference /9999   123456

Order Quantity: 200 doz   Delivery Date: 20/11/87

LABOUR COSTS

Number of pattern and special trim components	37

Pattern and pre-production costs:

Standard component cost element:	£25.00
X number of components gives:	£925.00

Divide by order quantity to give:

Pattern and pre-production costs: £4.625/doz (A)

Standard operations

Operations	Standard Hrs/Doz
Lockstitch collar at neck	0.10000
O/L Gauge sleeve to cuff	0.15000
Overlock shoulder seams	0.08200
Overlock Gauge in sleeves	0.18000
Overlock Bodice seams	0.15000
O/L Gauge skirts to bodice	0.20000
Lockstitch back seam	0.15200
Twin needle attach zip	0.11000
O/L back seam, att slider	0.20000
etc	0.67600
Total standard hours/doz	2.00000
Cost per dozen	£5.04000 (B)

Non-standard operations

Operation	Standard Hrs/Doz
Template collar	0.29000
Trim and turn collar	0.11000
Topstich collar and down at ft	0.05000
O/L att top collar w binding	0.20000
L/S seal hem and keyhole skt	0.15000
Total standard hours/doz	0.70000
Cost per dozen	£2.1000 (C)

Handling and inspection cost per dozen: £1.50000 (D)

TOTAL LABOUR COST PER DOZEN   £13.26500 (A + B + C + D)

MATERIALS

Fabric	Description	Colour	Rating	Cost/Metre	Cost Doz
02/17	legler BW c 4415 147	b&w	7.730	£3.43	£26.514
01/00	lining	00	4.040	£1.60	£6.464

Trim	Description	Colour	Rating	Cost/Unit	Cost/Doz
bt122	Button 2234		3	.011	$0.396
th56	CP thread 2234	Orange	36.56	2.56/10000	£0.112
zp199	YKK std zip	White	19.0cm	.90/m	£2.052
lb0991	Tag 2234		1	.12	£1.440
la447	lace ref 140677/8	Pink	7.0	.36	£2.520

Sundry	Description		Usage	Cost/Unit	Cost/Doz
Pk2234	Package ref 2234		1/12	.200	£0.200
Ht2234	Hanging tag 2234		1	.070	£0.840
ct001	3 doz carton		1/30	.540	£0.180

TOTAL MATERIALS COSTS	£40.718
FIXED ORDER COSTS (Administration, planning etc)	£267.000
Divided by order quantity gives Order cost per doz:	£1.335
TOTAL DIRECT COSTS (MATERIALS LABOUR AND ORDER)	£55.318

INDIRECT COSTS

Overhead absorption rate: 125% of labour costs

Overhead costs	£16.581
TOTAL COST PER DOZEN	**£71.899**

GROSS MARGIN REQUIRED   30%

GROSS PROFIT	£21.570
SALES PRICE	£93.469

Source: Apparel International April 1988

Assignments

1 Look in a current fashion magazine and see how many retail fashion garments you can find that have been influenced by the following:

   a) music
   b) films
   c) a personality

How have the manufacturers incorporated the features into the garments? Write a report choosing at least one example from each category with a different retailer for each.

2 *Sizing survey*

Go into the following stores, or close alternatives if there is not one near you.

   Marks & Spencer
   River Island
   Jaeger (or a Jaeger section (concession) in a department store)
   Dorothy Perkins or Burtons

In each one pick *one* style of garment which the shop is well stocked with.

   a) State the size range available (e.g. 8, 10, 12, 14).
   b) State the quantities of each size available in that style. Express these as percentages. You can draw up a bar chart or pie chart to illustrate this.
   c) State what type of customer you think they are aiming at with each size range of clothes.

3 *Complaints interviews*

Interview two friends, two neighbours and two people much older than yourself (lecturer, mother, grandfather, etc.). Ask them to tell you their most frequent complaints about garment make-up and sizing. Make lists of the commonest problems and of the more unusual ones. For each problem say how you feel they could either be avoided or put right.

4 Select a favourite garment and, using the technical size and specification chart in this chapter as a guide, complete as many details about the garment as you can. Remember to look inside for the wash/care instructions and to lay the garment flat on a table for measuring.

Chapter 5

THE
BUYERS

One of the most coveted careers in the fashion industry is that of the fashion buyer. Buyers are the powerful individuals who decide which styles we will have access to in the shops. The popular image of a buyer is of someone constantly flying to Paris and Milan for breakfast meetings and fashion shows! This is not so for the majority of buyers. They work closely with the merchandisers who organise the selling side and they all stay close to their ledgers and computer terminals, straying only to oversee production or delivery in Manchester or, occasionally perhaps, Macau or Hong Kong (see Chapter 2). Buyers and merchandisers work together to achieve profits for a retail organisation and to satisfy customer demands. Let us look at the various systems within which they have to function.

The primary aim of any retail company is to meet and satisfy changing consumer needs and to provide merchandise which the customer wants to buy, at a cost to the company which enables it to make maximum profit. Successful merchandising, therefore, can be said to involve six 'rights'. Retailers must aim to provide:

- the right product
- at the right price
- in the right quantity
- of the right quality (for the target market)
- in the right place (selling environment, store design, service and location)
- at the right time within fashion seasons (Consumer interest in certain areas of the fashion market can *turn on* or *turn off* within a matter of weeks.)

The organisation of buying

There are different types of buying, depending on the type of retail organisation. Multiples tend to buy centrally while department stores generally merge buying with the management of selling and operate local buying systems. However, the House of Fraser, John Lewis and others centralise some buying, especially for standard lines of merchandise. Co-operatives diversify by buying from CWS (The Co-operative Wholesale Society), or from local societies through local consortia or locally via managers. Independent stores (where the owner and manager may be one and the same person) will usually buy locally but, if there are a few branches, some lines may be bought in centrally.

Central buying

Advantages

- Discounts can be obtained for buying in bulk.
- The buyer has a special knowledge of the product.
- The buyer has a broader awareness of the market.
- The buyer is a highly skilled negotiator.
- Merchandise can be moved centrally and is therefore more flexible.
- The stores and their managers can concentrate on selling, achieving a higher rate of stock turnover through better sales techniques.

Disadvantages

- The specific consumer needs in any locality may be ignored.
- Warehousing and distribution costs increase.
- Local managers have less influence over the type of stock they carry and therefore may feel frustrated.

An organisation chart of a central buying department within a multiple retailer.

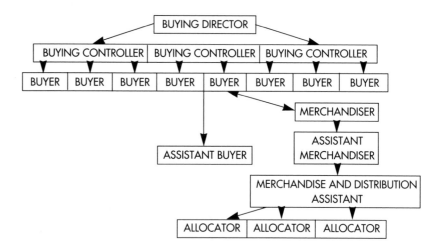

Local buying

Advantages

- The buyer knows the customer base well.
- The buyer has direct control over the stock in his or her department store.
- Stock can be held in store for easy replenishment.

Disadvantages

- Smaller orders attract less preferential terms, i.e. smaller discounts.
- The buyer has less specific product knowledge.
- There are more demands on the buyer's manager's time resulting in decreased efficiency.

An organisation chart of the local buying scenario within an independent retailer.

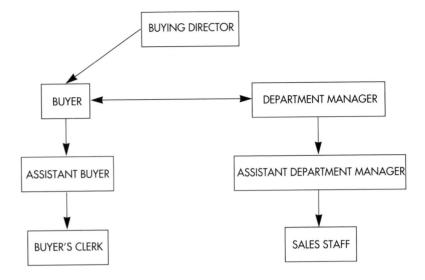

The buyer and department manager
may be the same person.

However, some smaller department stores and independents are members of AIS (Associated Independent Stores), which acts as a central buying resource and has its own label: Czarina.

The buyer

The buyer is a highly skilled individual who is usually supported by an assistant and also by a clerk. Their job is to acquire the right goods of the right quality and in the right quantity. To do this the buyer has to:

- research the market, fashion trends and new suppliers, keeping abreast of all developments
- maintain a reliable and appropriate supplier base
- make forecasts of stock and budget requirements
- select and buy in merchandise which is appropriate for the target consumer and which is within budget and profit margins set
- negotiate with suppliers to agree the best terms (delivery, price, discounts) and ensure profit margins are attained, and that current legislation is observed.
- maintain an acceptable level of quality throughout the range

To perform these functions well, a buyer needs to have:

- initiative and enthusiasm
- foresight and planning skills
- leadership and determination
- an understanding of finance
- interpersonal skills and integrity

The merchandiser

A merchandiser is also a highly skilled individual who has to perform many functions. The most important of these are to:

- make long-range plans and forecasts of sales, profit margins and stock products
- keep accurate records of goods bought, sales, returns, transfers and markdowns
- control the mark-up and margins, to cover expenses and to produce a profit in the buying budget
- maintain stock levels within a budget
- control what to buy and advise the buyer of what has been bought
- implement the company trading policy in merchandising terms, e.g. pricing policy
- assist with sales promotional activity by briefing relevant staff of stock assortments available

In order to be effective, a merchandiser needs to have:

- a sound undestanding of finance
- initiative and leadership
- entrepreneurial skills
- foresight and planning skills
- analytical ability

A merchandiser often controls a team of allocators, led by a senior allocator, whose job is to distribute goods to the right place, at the right time and in the right quantity.

Buying policy

A retailer's buying policy is closely related to the overall company strategy; it identifies the right goods for the right consumer by giving clear guidelines on the following aspects:

- types of goods and customer profile (age and socio-economic group – see page 67)
- number of lines
- assortment, in depth or breadth (see page 57)
- quality of goods
- fashion attitude
- degree of exclusivity

The buying policy therefore is the central factor involved in all buying decisions. The **buying cycle**, when complete, will affect and sometimes amend the buying policy through performance feedback. Essentially, though, it is the policy that determines the planning of the range.

An example of a typical buying cycle for a multiple retailer.

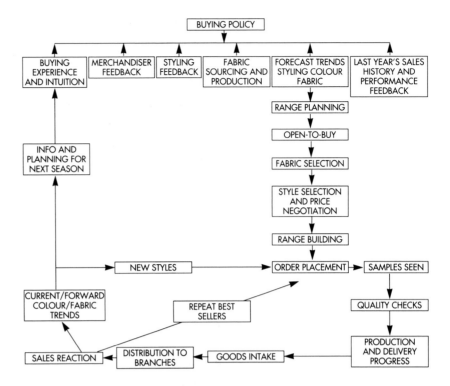

Range planning

The planning of a range can be broken down into separate tasks, although these often overlap each other.

Style prediction

A buyer's check-list

- Analyse last season's sales, in respect of:
    - styles
    - colour
    - fabric
    - details

    Which sold best or worst and in what stores?
- Assess the stage the style has reached in the fashion cycle by using this sales figure analysis. Use this to determine the need for restocking certain styles. For example, if optimum sales are reached at the height of a season, then the style has reached saturation point and there is no need for reinvestment.
- Assess outside influences such as:
    - a) the market, the economy, politics, technology. How do these factors influence the consumer?
    - b) the media, TV shows, films, music, popular personalities. Will consumers copy styles from TV stars, pop groups, etc. – the **emulation factor**?

Consultancy services

Many buyers buy in expertise either in person or through reports by companies such as Nigel French, Design Intelligence and Informoda, or through textile organisations who produce fibre-specific reports, such as Courtaulds, the International Wool Secretariat and the Cotton Institute.

Trade shows and exhibitions

Often buyers will visit a trade show for confirmation of forward trends and not necessarily to buy. This is especially true at fabric fairs and exhibitions aimed at the top end of the market, which can give a strong idea of trends to the buyer of mainstream merchandise.

Other sources of information

These include:

- trade magazines such as *DR The Fashion Business*, *Fashion Weekly* and *Womenswear Resources*
- trade directories like Yellow Pages, Kelly's and buyer's guides
- newspapers
- consumer magazines
- international magazines
- local competitors' windows and stock – to judge what is available and its impact
- his/her own store(s) – to listen to and observe customer preferences
- shops in other retail areas – to assess stock selections

Identifying sources of supply

Once information on styling has been compiled, a buyer begins to enquire into possible sources of supply. Some suppliers will be known to the buyer, but the buyer is constantly seeking new ideas, better merchandise and more competitive margins, so new suppliers will also be sought, especially if any existing supplier cannot satisfy some of the buyer's requirements. The suppliers fall into the following categories.

Manufacturers

They are a direct source of supply, mainly for larger stores and multiples, for example Marks & Spencer. The buyer will be able to control the order by specifying precisely to the manufacturer what is required. That control also exists over quantities, quality and delivery schedules. As this type of buying can take a long time to process – it starts approximately one year ahead of retailing – it can prove to be inflexible in satisfying some customer needs in terms of fashion styling.

Wholesalers

A wholesaler offers a quick response to fashion styling and often acts as a stock holder, so deliveries can sometimes take place within just a few weeks. The main advantage of using wholesalers is that they will break bulk orders into smaller parts for small or independent stores. Some wholesalers will also offer a 'cash and carry' facility via a showroom or stock house. These are found in areas like the East End of London and Manchester. They may, however, stipulate a minimum order, as this saves on their administrative costs. Special concessions like credit and discounts may not be available to the buyer until the wholesaler has traded with them for, say, two or three seasons. A disadvantage of wholesalers for the large retailer is that they are not useful for volume orders.

Importers

Importers are especially useful to a buyer who does not have the time or experience to buy direct from abroad. Most importers have their specialities such as Italian knitwear, Norwegian rainwear or cotton goods from Asia. The importer will not only act as an intermediary between the buyer and the supplier but will complete all the necessary importation documents, observing all legal restraints such as import duties and quotas. The skill of the importer enables the buyer to source overseas with minimum fuss, with fewer buying trips and with little or no knowledge of the supplier's language.

Agents and brokers

Agents sell goods on behalf of a company or companies. They only hold samples and do not own ranges or hold any stock. They work on a strict 'commission only' basis.

Open-to-buy

Once the sales targets for a period have been determined, the buyer's budget can be set. This budget is called the **open-to-buy**. An open-to-buy is calculated, often by computer, for the year or season and then broken down into smaller periods of time, usually months. It shows how much money has to be spent on stock to achieve the planned sales targets. The buyer sets the open-to-buy in consultation with the merchandiser.

With an open-to-buy in hand, the buyer can allocate this to an ideal stock plan, often called the **model stock plan** or the **range plan**. The other information which has been determined by this stage is styling information, and types and colours of fabrics required. A model stock plan for each style can be drafted so that by the time the buyer begins to negotiate with the supplier, the buyer is clear about what is within the budget and what stock levels will be sufficient.

A stock plan for the dresses department of West End Girls is given at the top of p. 56. The categories of choices are clearly indicated; these will obviously change seasonally, according to the dictates of fashion.

An advert to attract agents to represent a wholesale fashion company.

West End Girls – Dresses

Open-to-buy at cost price £10,000. Autumn transition.

Styles

45% classic: coat dresses, tunic, shift style	= £4500
25% fashion: prints, belted, large-collared	= £2500
15% basic: T-shirts, jersey	= £1500
15% quality: occasion dresses, dresses with jackets	= £1500

Colours

rose red	royal blue	cream
emerald green	black	beige

Fabrics

poly/viscose blend	poly/cotton blend
100% cotton	100% wool
wool/polyester blend	

Cost prices (average) £10, £12, £15, £20, £25

Sizes 10, 12, 14, 16 (ratio 1 : 3 : 4 : 2)

Using the outlined parameters, the model stock plan below has been calculated to represent a broad selection of garments in price band, size and price.

The model stock plan for fashion dresses might then look like this; the plan is expressed in units, that is numbers of garments, not actual cost.

West-End Girls – Fashion dresses

Total budget for fashion dresses = £2,500

(A) 25% for £12 units = £625 ÷ 12 = 52 (£624)
(B) 30% for £15 units = £750 ÷ 15 = 50
(C) 45% for £20 units = £1125 ÷ 20 = 56 (£1120)
(D) TOTAL UNITS (£6 under budget) = 158

Size ratio = 10:12:14:16 / 1:3:4:2 (10%:30%:40%:20%)
There are equal ratios on style and fabric.
(N.B. if rounding does occur it is in favour of sizes 12 and 14 or for a balance of colours across all sizes with a preference for blue and black)

		PRINTS		BELTED		LARGE COLLARED		
PRICE	Size	Red/Green Poly/Viscose	Blue/Black Poly/Cotton	Red 100% Cotton	Black Poly/Cotton	Black Poly/Viscose	Blue Poly/Cotton	TOTALS
£12	10	1	1	1	1	1	0	5
	12	2	3	3	3	3	2	16
	14	3	4	3	4	4	3	21
	16	1	2	2	2	2	1	10
							(A)	52
£15	10	1	1	0	1	1	1	5
	12	2	3	2	3	2	3	15
	14	3	3	3	4	3	4	20
	16	2	2	1	1	2	2	10
							(B)	50
£20	10	0	1	1	1	1	1	5
	12	2	3	3	3	3	3	17
	14	3	4	4	4	4	4	23
	16	1	2	2	2	2	2	11
							(C)	56
							(D)	158

Model stock plan checklist
* The units are worked out from the *total budget* using the *price factors*. * All figures are *rounded* to the nearest decimal place.
* All figures are *totalled* and can be used to check back. * *Statements* are made on percentages, ratios and rounding.

The example shows that fashion dresses are stocked in *breadth*, that is in a wide selection of colours, prices, sizes, fabrics and so on. To stock in *depth* would typically be to offer something more basic on a larger scale, for example jeans, one style, three sizes, one price. To stock a fashion item in *depth* you have to be confident that it will sell well. To stock in *breadth* offers fashion consumers choice and encourages them to buy. It leads (hopefully!) to this sort of 'decision': 'I just can't decide between the red and green print dress and the black belted dress – they're both so fashionable. I'll just have to have both of them!'

Product choices: brands vs own brands

The decision whether to buy branded merchandise or use a company label is often encompassed in the buying policy.

Own branding

There are two types of **own branding**.

a) *Integrated*   This is a vertically organised operation within the company and is not sub-contracted. There is good control over quality and delivery to stores as there are no intermediaries. The Jaeger brand is a good example of this type.

b) *Independent contracting*   The goods are sub-contracted out to CMT units in this country or abroad, but manufactured according to specific quality and size specifications. Marks & Spencer and Top Shop use this method.

The advantages of own branding are numerous. They include:

- easy ordering for manufacturers
- lower costs so profit margins are higher
- greater price choice for consumers
- better use of floor space for the retailer
- controls on delivery
- controls on quality
- enhanced corporate identity and greater customer loyalty.

The disadvantages are:

- the strong image of some proprietary brands
- necessity of large orders
- out-selling of successful brands by own brands – this will upset other suppliers
- long lead times (from order to delivery)
- slow response to fashion trends

Brands

Manufacturers often identify their version of a product by a name, that is a **brand name**. Some brands, especially if they are in the sports, leisure, lingerie or casual wear sectors of the market, have a high intrinsic 'cult' value to the customer. In these cases, no store's own brand can compete with them side-by-side. Levi 501s, Nike trainers, Ray-ban wayfarer sunglasses and Gossard wonderbras are all in this category.

Pricing decisions

Selling price

When retailers work out how much to sell a garment for, they have to consider how much they paid for it, including VAT – the **cost price** – and how much profit they want to make – the **gross margin**. They may decide they want to have a gross margin of 60 per cent on dresses as a whole. This means they can sell some at a lower profit, provided others are priced high enough to give an average of 60 per cent.

The **gross margin** is expressed as a percentage of the selling price. So an item sold at £15.99, with a cost price of £7.50, yields a profit of £8.49, or a gross margin of approximately 53 per cent.

$$\frac{£\ 8.49}{£15.99} \times 100\% = 53.09\%$$

The **markup**, on the other hand, is the percentage of the cost price which needs to be added to achieve the selling price. So, in the above example, the markup will be approximately 113 per cent.

$$\frac{£8.49}{£7.50} \times 100\% = 113.20\%$$

Price pointing

A number of prices for selling are identified before buying begins. This trains the buyer to 'buy backwards' to achieve margins, rather than adding a uniform markup which, when applied to various cost prices, will result in a non-uniform selling price selection. So there is a limited number of distinct selling prices, for example £9.99, £15.99, £19.99, regardless of variations in cost price.

There are some psychological aspects to be considered when pricing clothes. Psychological prestige is bestowed on a garment and its wearer by a price in round figures. It makes the article appear more exclusive. It says, 'If you have money, you don't quibble over pennies'. An example would be a Giorgio Armani jacket priced at £850. The psychological value of a garment is reduced by the use of odd pricing, which makes a garment appear to be cheaper. An example might be: 'Shirts – only £9.99'. In this case all the shirts are under £10 but only just. The retailer hopes you will convince yourself that you paid 'about £9' not £10 for the item!

Marking down

An unavoidable fact of life in fashion retailing is that, as garments reach obsolescence, they have to be marked down in price to clear or else they remain as **terminal stocks**, unsaleable, and a burden to the future of the open-to-buy figure. The more fashionable or faddish the garment, the higher the markdown has to be to avoid high terminal stocks.

There are various reasons why a garment may have to be marked down.

- It may simply have been overpriced.
- It may not be a suitable item for that particular store to keep (merchandising error).
- The buyer may have made an error of judgement in selecting it (buying error).
- The buyer may have set a high initial margin to accommodate a possible markdown.
- The markdown may be by percentage (e.g. 10% off) or by value (e.g. £2 off). Either way, margins are diminished.
- The supplier may have agreed to cover the cost of part of the markdown. This is known as 'supplier-funded markdown or discount' (SFM or SFD). Once all markdowns and discounts have been taken into account, the margin which results is known as the 'net achieved margin'.

Computerised feedback

Most orders are processed through computer and so are most sales. There are few fashion retailers who have not seen the advantages of computer applications. There are two ways in which information about sales can be fed back.

EPOS

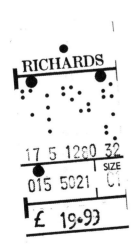

A Kimball tag. This records sales and stock information and acts as a price and size label, too.

Electronic point-of-sale (EPOS) is the term used when the till is linked to a computer network, often used in conjunction with barcode scanners. It is common in supermarkets and department stores, and it is becoming more widespread. The sales information is then directly relayed to central buying offices, so that buyers and merchandisers get direct feedback about the relative success of their purchases.

Ticketing

Some other methods of **ticketing** the merchandise provide the same results for the central buyer and merchandiser. One of the most widely used systems is the 'Kimball tag'. Each tag has four parts, the first two to record sales, the others to record re-sales and returns. Each part of the tag will contain a combination of information, for example manufacturer's code, department code, style code, week number, size, colour code and selling price.

Assignments

1 Draft a model stock plan in units for the men's shirts department using the following data:

Planned investment = £30,000

Cost Prices	Percentage of stock
£10	60%
£15	40%

Colours	
White	35%
Blue	30%
Grey	35%

Neck sizes	
14½	25%
15	25%
15½	30%
16	20%

2 Visit *one* store from each list:

a) QS
   What She Wants
   What Everyone Wants
   Mark One *or* local discount fashion store
b) Jaeger (store or concession)
   Whistles
   Phase Eight
   Jigsaw *or* local upmarket fashion store

Write out for each what you think their buying policy is, including a profile of their ideal customer. In your opinion, what are the differences between the two buying policies?

Chapter 6

THE
SELLERS

Retailers of fashion

In recent years there have been many changes in the way fashion has been sold. The key factors involved are related to the economy, to demography and to standards of living. The most noticeable changes are:

- more high fashion and designer ranges
- wider and diversified ranges
- more casual clothing
- more self-selection
- more off-the-peg clothing
- decline in outerwear
- growth and diversification in childrenswear
- market shifts away from teenage clothing to an older more upmarket image
- concession retailing (see page 64) becoming important and store design becoming a central part of selling

Let us look at different kinds of retailer and their characteristics.

Independents

These are retailers with fewer than ten branches. Most of them, in fact, are sole traders with only one or two outlets. They offer convenience and the 'personal touch' to their customers and often specialise in certain categories of clothing. Many older customers prefer shopping for clothes in independents because the staff or owner get to know them and their needs, thus bringing more pleasure to shopping there.

Multiples

Multiples consist of a chain of shops, or several chains, owned by a large parent company; for example, Miss Selfridge is part of the Sears Group.

There are two categories of multiple: those which specialise, for example Mothercare (mother and baby clothing and goods), Olympus Sports (sports goods), Top Man (young men's fashion) and those which cater for a variety of customers, for example Marks and Spencer, BHS and Woolworths. All multiples have the following characteristics:

- They buy centrally and in bulk.
- They have other centralised functions such as training, personnel, marketing, display.
- They occupy prime sites, like high street or shopping centre locations.
- They promote a very strong corporate image through store design and packaging to own branding.
- They usually have a high turnover of goods.
- They can have additional customer benefits, e.g. cafés (Next, Habitat), credit cards (M&S, Burton Group, Sears Group), mother and baby facilities (Boots, Mothercare). These benefits encourage customer loyalty.

Department stores

These are usually large stores which sell a variety of goods, not only clothes. There are three different types.

Independents

These are often family-owned and include stores like Eaden Lilley in Cambridge and Beales in Bournemouth.

Small multiples

These operate a small number of branches, for example Fenwick, Bentalls and Allders.

Large multiples

These include the John Lewis Partnership, the House of Fraser and Debenhams. They have the following features:

- They occupy prime sites.
- They offer a range of extra facilities to customers such as restaurants, credit cards, toilets, in-store banking.
- They can offer concessions to other retailers, notably in the fashion area, for example Jaeger, Windsmoor and Alexon.
- They have a strong corporate image, even if the store operates under several different names, like the John Lewis Partnership.
- Some functions, like buying, marketing and training of personnel, are centralised.

Superstores

Superstores have recently 'strengthened their offer' in respect of men's, women's and children's clothing. This means that they have expanded these departments. Notable examples are Tesco (Home and Wear) and Asda (By George). Superstores have the following characteristics:

- They buy centrally, and centralise most other functions.
- They are large (up to 2,500 square metres) and usually occupy out-of-town sites with adequate parking facilities.

- Most of the store is on ground level.
- They aim to have a very high turnover of stock.
- They can offer many extra facilities to customers, such as:
    - cafés and restaurants
    - toilets and mother-and-baby rooms
    - banking and cash points
    - crèches and children's playgrounds

Discount stores

Discount stores thrive on rejected fashion merchandise of the sort that is rejected or cancelled due to poor quality or late delivery. Examples are QS, What She Wants and Mark One. Discount stores have these characteristics:

- They have a high turnover with low margins.
- They are often in 'secondary' sites close to the high street, or at a location with lower rents.
- The shop fittings are very basic, with clear signs to facilitate self-service.

Co-operative stores

The co-operative retail movement started in Britain in the nineteenth century. Suppliers, employees and some customers are all technically speaking 'members' of the society and get shared benefits from trading. They have survived, despite the growth of multiples and department stores, but have often adapted to present a more up-to-date image to the customer. Co-op clothing still has a down-market image, however. The following points distinguish these stores:

- They are 'owned' by regional societies, for example the Royal Arsenal Co-op and Co-op Leos.
- They are in both prime-site and secondary locations.
- They offer a very varied number of services from funeral services to banking and insurance.
- Some functions, like buying, are centralised through the Co-operative Wholesale Society, but most other functions are regional.

Mail order

Mail order has increased in recent years, especially since it has been supplemented by telephone ordering and more recently by computer/TV ordering. Many new catalogues have entered the market providing a more specialised service which can be more directly targeted to the right consumer, for example the Next Directory and Scotcade. Traditional mail order catalogues are run by specialist catalogue houses such as Freemans or Littlewoods. Mail order has the following characteristics:

- Increased competition among mail order houses means better service and faster delivery.

- As catalogues come out only twice a year there is less flexibility in responding to consumer demand, although some catalogues produce special seasonal brochures, for example Next's Christmas Directory.
- They spend heavily on advertising but they save even more on lower overhead costs.

Concessions

A concession is a letting-out of in-store space by a retailer to another retailer, for example Jaeger within Harvey Nichols, Knightsbridge. The concession giver receives the benefit of increased line diversification without the risks attached. Certain concession names act as an attraction to customers who look for prestige labels. Concessions are distinguished by the following features:

- There is a concession agreement which offers a degree of protection to both parties.
- Concessions are often let out for a fixed percentage of turnover, and a minimum percentage is guaranteed.
- The concessionaire only has to provide fixtures and fittings, point of sale material, merchandise and staff.
- There are rental positions, such as Hyper Hyper or Kensington Market, which charge rental per square foot, although some department stores charge a fixed rental *plus* a percentage of the turnover.
- They are good at targeting prestige customers in specialist merchandise areas, younger customers and frequent store users.

Franchises

Franchising is a relatively new development in retailing. It is 'the granting of sole selling rights within a geographic area'. The most successful franchises are in fast food, but fashion is fast catching up. Examples are Oasis Trading, Dash, Benetton (no royalties/fees) and Body Shop. Franchises typically have the following characteristics:

- The franchising company provides merchandise packaging and point-of-sale promotional material.
- The franchisee pays a fixed franchise fee or a percentage of turnover.
- Franchisees are often helped in finding a location for the store.
- Franchisees are often given specialised training.
- The franchising company offers the most valuable package of a tried and tested retail formula and the licence to operate the franchise and use the trade-mark.

Market segmentation in fashion retailing

The trend towards market segmentation is strongest in fashion retailing, especially amongst the specialist multiple retailers. Because people regard buying clothes as an extension of their lifestyle and therefore their personality, they can be more easily identified not only according to age and socio-economic grouping, but also according to their attitudes.

Major segmentation factors

Age   Miss Selfridge, for example, targets the 15–19-year-old consumer.

Lifestyle   Some retailers, like Next and Principles, concentrate on working women who want workable separates, that is business clothes plus classic styling.

Physical characteristics   Stores which cater for the non-averitic customer include Evans for the larger woman and High & Mighty for the larger man.

Demographics   The population distribution determines what stores are placed where, their size, and what merchandise they sell.

Fashion attitudes   The study of these is called psychographics. There are descriptors for each fashion attitude, such as 'fashion active', 'individualistic' or 'contemporary'.

Label   The continuing trend towards buying labelled or branded goods has made multiples like Benetton and The Gap more viable.

Socio-economic groupings   Harrods, for example, concentrates on customers from the A/B socio-economic group whilst Etam concentrates on C1 and C2 customers (see the chart below).

Group	Socio-economic group	% of population
A	Professional / upper middle	6
B	Professional / middle	7
C1	Non-manual / lower middle	18
C2	Manual / skilled working	37
D	Manual / semi / unskilled working	22
E	Pensioners / casual workers / unemployed	10

Source: R. Cox & P. Brittain, *Retail Management*, 1988.

Target market segmentation of retail consumers by psychographics (attitude).

	Age	Spending power	Fashion awareness	Description	Examples of retailers	Market share	Fashion Attitude
Pioneer							
Street	18–30	Low	Very high	Leader/Faddish	'Street' Hyper-Hyper	Less than 1%	Novel
Designer	25–40	Very high		Leader/Faddish	Browns Hobbs		
Imitator							
	18–25	Low/medium	High	Close follower	Miss Selfridge Top Shop Top Man ↓	15%	Novel adapted for price
Evolver	25–40	Medium/high	Medium	Contemporary	Next ↑ Solo Hornes New catalogues Independents ↓	20%	Restrained
Backseat	25+	Medium	Medium/low	Acquiescent	M&S ↑ BHS Mail order ↓	50%	Established
Basement	25+	Low	Low	Indifferent	Discount stores Market stalls	10%	Residual

Source: Kurt Salmon Associates.

Target market segmentation (womenswear) of
retail consumers by age, socio-economic
grouping and other factors (1990).

	Marks & Spencer	BHS	Littlewoods	Dorothy Perkins	Top Shop	Next	Richards	C&A	Dept store	Mail order*	Market stall
Base: women	583	257	212	188	144	111	97	265	189	314	156
	%	%	%	%	%	%	%	%	%	%	%
All	57	25	21	18	14	11	10	26	19	31	15
15–19	34	10	12	36	48	19	6	26	11	23	23
20–24	48	16	7	39	33	12	22	24	19	40	22
25–34	52	37	16	29	19	11	7	34	17	40	21
35–44	64	29	27	19	8	16	13	32	16	36	19
45–54	64	30	32	9	4	5	10	28	20	27	10
55–64	54	24	17	5	10	3	3	28	15	27	13
65+	52	15	25	2	3	2	5	10	16	26	3
AB	72	25	16	22	13	18	16	17	24	15	3
C1	62	26	19	18	17	11	12	24	21	37	14
C2	55	30	24	18	15	7	9	32	13	35	20
DE	43	16	22	14	12	5	4	23	12	29	15
London/TVS	62	29	20	12	13	12	12	21	21	31	14
Anglia/Central	54	17	26	23	15	9	10	23	11	30	17
Harlech/TSW	49	23	12	23	16	5	5	20	8	29	15
Yorkshire/Tyne Tees	50	24	12	11	14	6	5	32	14	30	16
Granada	59	27	29	23	20	7	14	32	17	39	18
Scotland	49	20	36	21	8	10	6	24	19	27	7
Working	64	29	22	23	17	12	16	31	20	33	18
Not working	47	19	22	15	15	8	4	21	12	32	14
Retired	52	22	12	3	3	–	–	15	20	24	4
Married	58	27	22	18	12	8	10	27	18	34	16
Not married	49	18	20	16	18	10	6	21	14	26	13
Children	48	25	19	24	18	11	9	30	12	36	23
No children	59	23	22	13	12	7	9	22	19	29	10

* Including Next Directory

Source: BMRB/Mintel

Assignments

1 Choose a retail area close to you (where you work, your high street or the shopping centre). Make a map with all the retail outlets and then make a colour-coded key to illustrate the stores by category. The categories are:

    department stores
    multiples
    independents
    franchises
    co-ops
    superstores
    discount stores

Then make a number-coded key to illustrate which stores sell:

    womenswear
    menswear
    childrenswear

You can further illustrate your map by working out the percentage in each group or category and making a bar chart or pie chart for each group.

2 Write an 'ideal customer profile' for three specialist multiple retailers detailed on your map. Describe:

    a) their residential location
    b) their fashion attitude
    c) their socio-economic group
    d) their typical job
    e) their typical leisure activities

3 Write a script of an imaginary advert to be transmitted by your local commercial radio station for one of the stores outlined in Assignment 1. Make sure that the script of the advert truly reflects the attitudes of the person you described in your customer profile in Assignment 2. You can record the advert onto a cassette and play it to friends and colleagues to discover whether you have hit the target customer 'on the nail'!

Chapter 7

THE
PROMOTERS

Fashion journalists

Working for a wide range of titles in newspapers and magazines and in the media generally, fashion journalists today no longer see their role as one of straight reportage. More and more, especially in women's consumer magazines, the fashion journalists see it as their task to inform their readership and to educate and lead them towards adopting new ideas. In some magazines, like *Vogue* or *Elle*, the editorial tone of some fashion articles veers towards being dictatorial while in others it is just mildly persuasive.

Types of media

Fashion journalists work for various organs, the main ones being:

- national newspapers, daily/evening/Sunday (e.g. *The Times*, *The Guardian*, *The Observer*)
- regional newspapers, daily/evening (e.g. *The Evening Standard*, *The Scotsman*, *Liverpool Echo*)
- local/provincial newspapers and free sheets (e.g. *Hackney Gazette*, *Ilford Recorder*)
- magazines/periodicals: weekly/general (e.g. *Radio Times* and *TV Times*); special interest (e.g. *Bella*, *Woman's Own*); monthly/general (e.g. *Prima*, *Vogue*, *Elle*)
- trade press, weekly/monthly and technical (e.g. *DR The Fashion Business*, *Apparel*)
- radio: national BBC, regional/local BBC and commercial
- television: national and regional programmes (e.g. *The Clothes Show*); national and regional news (e.g. TV-AM); cable and satellite

Sources of information

It is possible to check information about various types of media, for example advertising rates and circulation figures. The main sources of such information are:

- the Audit Burea of Circulations (ABC), which verifies publishers' circulation claims twice a year
- press guides, including Kellys, Willings, Benns, Pims/PNA and Brad (British Rate and Data – for advertising information), all of which can be found in reference and specialist libraries

Sources which provide up-to-date or specialist information or news include:

- the Central Office of Information (COI), a government information service which supplies a lot of overseas publications
- news and feature agencies, which 'sell' news stories and features to the press (e.g. Reuters, Associated Press (AP) and Inter Press Service (IPS))
- teletext news, film clip and information services (e.g. Oracle, Ceefax, Visnews and Prestel)

Fashion public relations

Fashion PR is a very new industry offshoot. It is broadly acknowledged that it was pioneered in this country by Lynne Franks, who first started by getting publicity for her husband, Paul Howie, who owned a shop in London's Covent Garden. As the success of both ventures grew, so did Lynne Franks' client list. Although Lynne Franks PR and her contemporaries are overshadowed by corporate PR concerns such as Shandwick Publications, the smaller trendier fashion PR company often wins out in gaining fashion clients as they have a detailed and specialist knowledge of the market. Although notable PR companies such as Jean Bennett and Lynne Franks handle prestigious clients like Naf Naf (UK) and Jean Paul Gaultier, respectively, many fashion companies will choose to have an in-house PR department or person.

Let us now examine the activities which a PR company engages in on behalf of a client.

Getting editorial space

This is more authoritative than advertising space; if a magazine or newspaper endorses a product in pictures or words then it is as good as sold. Look out for 'Vogue Cards' in high-class stores. The PR account executive contacts the appropriate media outlet and convinces the fashion editor/writer that the product is perfect for a feature or for use in a 'photo shoot'. The PR assistant will then label and book out the relevant sample of merchandise to the magazine, and in most cases will deliver it personally, making sure that the right person gets the goods. Once the sample has been seen and photographed, it will be returned to the PR office stockroom and booked in.

Once the editorial is published, cuttings will be retained by the account executive in order to show his/her boss or the client (if he/she is working for a PR agency) that adequate press coverage is being gained.

Press releases

Especially for new products or new promotions, a press release will be sent to a carefully targeted press audience in order to secure maximum coverage. They are often produced on eye-catching paper or in stunning folders. However, a press release on its own is not usually enough. It needs to be followed up with many enthusiastic phone calls urging the recipient to act on it.

A press release has the following format:

Name of company   Release
Date
Address
Telephone number

HEADLINE IN CAPS UNDERLINED

The text consists of double-spaced copy on one-sided paper only. The pages are numbered with the word 'more' put at the end of each page until the story ends, when the word 'end' is put. The content tells the reader all the details: *who, when, what, where* and *why*. Fashion photographs can also be enclosed with the release. Photographs are clear, often black and white, easily reproducible, 8 in. × 10 in. glossy prints. Loosely attached to the back of each print will be a piece of paper with a clear description of the photograph.

END

A press release for Levi 501 jeans gets the reader in the mood and provides appropriate visuals of the product.

Press releases can be issued in advance of a situation or for immediate use.

LEVI'S 'NEW DEAL' COMMERCIAL

Levi Strauss (UK) Limited, brand leader of the denim market, is investing in Wall Street for the latest Levi's 501 commercial.
Conceived by Levi's advertising agency Bartle Bogle Hegarty, directed by Hugh Johnson of Ridley Scott Associates and art directed by Arthur Max, the commercial brings a new dimension to the world of high finance. Shot in a specially constructed set at a Los Angeles studio, the ad captures the atmosphere of a busy stockbrokers' trading room, and is set to "The Joker" by The Steve Miller Band.

Called 'Great Deal' the commercial opens on a lift indicator panel, and a group of people waiting for it. The lift arrives; the doors open; the waiting passengers stand back in amazement. Out of the lift emerges a cool looking motorcyclist wearing sunglasses, leather jacket, denim shirt and Red Tab 501's, and riding a gleaming Harley Davidson. He removes his sunglasses and takes in the scene, rides slowly past an astonished security guard and continues round the hectic trading room, bringing the place to a complete standstill. Stunned female dealers bestow on him looks that are a mixture of disbelief and approval while their male counterparts throw him looks of grudging admiration.

He stops in front of girl who is engrossed in negotiations on two telephones. He pulls a pair of 501's from inside his leather jacket and throws them onto her desk. The girl looks up in surprise, but then she smiles, stands up, drops the skirt of her suit to the floor and slides into her 501's. Loosening her hair she tosses her head, throws caution to wind and climbs onto the back of the bike. The trading room is brought back to life by the thunderous applause of gaping dealers. The couple are last seen riding into the sunset over Manhattan's 59th Street Bridge. The super reads "Levi's 501's — The Original Workwear".

The commercial forms part of Levi's £6m marketing spend for 1990 and can be seen for the first time on July 4 on national TV and cinema in 40 second and 60 second versions respectively.

- END -

Photo-shoot

The PR company may organise fashion photo-shoots for their clients' merchandise. These photos can be used for press releases and/or for promotional brochures/catalogues.

The PR account executive will make all the necessary arrangements with regard to using the merchandise. He/she will:

- collect the merchandise and accessories
- book in the merchandise and accessories
- arrange insurance

The PR account executive will also make the necessary creative decisions about the shoot. These include selecting:

- a theme
- a photographer (via agencies)
- models (using model books from agencies)
- the location/studio
- stylists (hairdressers, make-up, etc.)

The smooth running of the shoot is then up to the PR account executive, who also has to return the merchandise and get the prints ready for the client to select.

Press launch

Another sort of PR activity is the press launch or preview, an approach which is particularly relevant for new products. There is no set format but 'lavish' or 'stylish' are key words here. For example, a 'champagne and bagel brunch' in a canalside warehouse studio could be arranged to launch a new range of American designer-label classic separates. Food, drink and giveaways feature heavily in these publicity activities.

Fashion shows

The fashion show is a promotional activity which is much hyped and adored within the fashion industry. It is probably the single most glamorous activity in the fashion world, with a high concentration of pressure, theatre and artistic temperament. PR agencies organise most of the fashion shows that have a good reputation, often employing specialist fashion show producers and stagers. Some fashion shows can be in-house to, say, retail outlets and produced by a fashion show producer or internal management. Most shows these days are informal and set to pacey music. Gone are the days of numbered models, ushered in by a commentator, although some couture houses still do use these. The fashion show producer will plan a budget to cover the following:

rent for hire of venue	models' fees
transport	food and drink

staging/catwalk	music
electricians/lighting	insurance
video and PA	stylists (hair and make-up)
prop hire	dressers
tickets and programmes	security

The producer will then appoint teams to organise various aspects of the show:

the fitting and styling of merchandise

the theme and sequence of scenes

rehearsal arrangements

dresser co-ordination

prompters to get models on and off stage on time

the music sequence

The overall show should ideally last between 30 and 45 minutes. If it is longer than that most audiences start to fall asleep or leave!

The PR company, or in-house PR, then only have to publicise the event in the usual way, with a press release or invitation and a telephone call to remind important individuals about the show. As fashion shows are usually enjoyable, the problem is usually in turning people away, not in getting them in. Fashion shows, although expensive to stage, are one of the best aids to selling and can stimulate a lot of good publicity.

Styling

Stylists put the finishing touches to many glossy images. They prepare a range and finalise all the necessary trends. Most stylists work in relation to photographic work and will arrange accessories and a range of clothes and 'the look' required. Stylists may also arrange an appropriate hair stylist and make-up stylist for the job. Stylists also work on fashion shows and press launches if it is considered appropriate by the fashion show producer. A stylist will find all the accessories for a fashion shoot not only to complement 'the look' but also to suit the price range of the target consumer.

Fashion consultancies

Consultancies can operate on two levels:

- as publishers of style prediction reports and of retail and international fashion reports
- as consultants on range planning, producing, for example, specialist forward information packages

In their publishing role, they may use many people on a self-employed basis, such as illustrators, copywriters and so on. As consultants, on the other hand, they may charge a fixed fee for their advice on a daily basis. Well-known consultancy companies include Nigel French, Design Intelligence, Faces and Carlin International.

An example of a prediction report for women's lingerie by Nigel French.

LINGERIE FEATURE

RETURN TO A NEW FEMININITY AND THE SENSUAL TOUCH

NIGEL French

Looking at today's lingerie offering, the real catalyst for change within the market can be traced back to the mid-eighties when top American designer, Calvin Klein shocked the fashion world by suggesting that women might like to abandon their traditional frills and lace for their boyfriend's or husband's briefs! The revolution began and Calvin Klein became the focus of lingerie manufacturers worldwide as lookalike brands began to change the shape of women's underpinnings.

Simple jersey pieces by Calvin Klein have become new basics. For the season ahead (and Autumn/Winter 1992) Lycra and Lycra blended jersey fabrics will continue to impact the underwear/outerwear market. But within the 'no frills' market a new key item has appeared. The body-suit pioneered by American Designer, Donna Karan has now become a seasonal staple – layered underskirts and separates. The bodysuit has created a new niche within the lingerie market as a fashionable and versatile classification at all levels in a variety of fabrications and colours.

Moving forward, megastar Madonna, along with French designer, Jean Paul Gaultier, are having the greatest influence on the market, bringing sexy lingerie back out of the closet. Bustiers, waspies and '50's style boned bra tops are now essential partywear at the younger end of the market – particularly when teamed with a straight skirt.

The importance of fashion prints have also transformed our traditional perceptions of the market. Outerwear prints now add a new dimension to both lingerie and sleepwear.

For the contemporary consumer fashion lingerie is moving back towards a new femininity. We have gone full circle.

Helped by the new fabric and fibre technology which has led to the development of fine quality stretch laces, 'peach skin' finishes to synthetics and washable properties for silk, a change is sweeping the entire apparel industry and the lingerie offer must follow.

Important details for Autumn/Winter 1991/92 will include a re-emphasis on soft touch fabrics, velour and velvet being particularly important. Drape effects and stretch lace will add the feminine touch, along with traditional lingerie colours like powder blue and blush pink which will be mirrored in blouses and tops.

Key colours for autumn will focus on a new pastel level – summer colours for winter. A soft floral bouquet of celandine, violet, carnation pink, lavender and rose work together to create a new sensitivity and sensuality.

It is very much a season of contrasts, hard edged or soft. Styling themes for the season follow three paths – the continuing sportive theme updated with new pastel shades; the structured, bone sculptured look using pearlised sheen fabrics; and the soft, fluid femininity. Pink and lavender caste tones will be the key statement, but for more dramatic stories, red, peony and fuchsia will dominate.

One common denominator through the contrasting styles will be the creative use of new fabric and fibre technology pioneered by Japanese convertors, providing new handles and finishes and the inspiration for the resulting choice in sensual silhouettes.

NFEL provide a wide range of forecasting and consultancy services to the textile industry. For further information please contact: Liz Deeks, Nigel French Enterprises Ltd, 55 Colebrooke Row, London Nl 8AF Tel: 071-354 8001. Fax: 071-354 5004.

Assignments

1   Imagine you have the job of launching a new product into the market. Write a press release to reflect its qualities. Choose one of the following products:

   a)   a men's underwear range called 'Smartypants'
   b)   a new women's international designerwear shop in Islington, London, called 'Globalwise'
   c)   a new childrenswear collection for 2–8-year-olds, to be sold in superstores and called 'Tot it all up'
   d)   a British designer perfume for men and women called 'Signature'

   Remember to take into account the key points outlined on page 72 and to type your press release – or produce it on a wordprocessor if you have access to one.

2   Collect fashion articles from the following:

   a national daily paper
   a weekly women's magazine
   a monthly fashion magazine
   a fashion trade journal

   Examine the journalists' styles and list their similarities and differences. Do they:

   a)   fully describe the subject in clear language?
   b)   use jargon or specialist language?
   c)   offer statements of fact?
   d)   offer statements of opinion?

   Give examples in your answer of the above from the articles you have collected. State which style you prefer and why.

Chapter 8

THE
LAW

There are numerous Acts of Parliament which any person in business should be acquainted with, but for this context it will suffice to summarise the current legislation surrounding the sale of goods, on which copyright law has already been outlined in Chapter 2.

Sale of Goods Act 1979

This Act applies to all goods you can pay for, but not to services like cleaning. There are three key features of the Act.

1 Goods sold should be of *merchantable quality*. In other words, they should be in a saleable condition, not marked or imperfect in any way. The customer can only reject the goods if the fault has not been pointed out before the sale. If the customer is aware of the fault before money changes hands, the customer has implicitly accepted that fact, made an offer of money, and therefore a contract has been made.

2 Goods sold should be *fit for the purpose* for which they are intended. So if you buy a beautifully made shirt with no buttons on it, which means the shirt cannot be worn, or if a coat marked 'autumn raincoat' lets in the rain, then neither one is fit for its purpose.

3 Goods sold should *correspond to their description*, so if a woollen sweater carries a label which says 'Handmade by craftsmen' when in fact it was made by machine, then the description is untrue. The same applies to trousers marked '32 in inside leg' when in fact they measure 30 in. In cases like these the customer has the right to apply for a full cash refund. No retailer has the right to ask the customer to accept a credit note or alternative goods, unless, of course, the customer agrees to it. Customers do not have to produce a receipt or any other proof of purchase other than the goods themselves. Claims against retailers can be made up to six years after the original purchase.

Trade Descriptions Acts 1968, 1972

Under the 1968 Act penalties are incurred by anybody who either uses a false trade description or sells something with a false trade description or gives misleading information about any goods for sale. The 1972 Act stipulates that the country of origin for most imported goods should be clearly labelled, especially if they are made under licence for a UK company or if they appear to have been made in the UK, for example Guernsey wool sweaters, which may be made abroad in the Guernsey style.

The following features must be described accurately:

- size
- method of manufacture
- fibre composition, e.g. 100% wool
- purpose
- other physical characteristics, e.g. A-line skirt
- approval by outside bodies, e.g. Design Council Award
- date of manufacture
- name of manufacturer
- other history, e.g. secondhand

Origin Marking Orders 1981

These require goods to be labelled with the country of origin of the main processor or manufacturer, not where finishing, such as embroidery, took place. So a blouse can be embroidered in India and constructed in Manchester, yet still be labelled 'Made in the UK'. Retailers must either label the goods or hang a swing ticket, and wholesalers and suppliers must supply buyers with the 'country of origin' information at least before the date of delivery of the goods.

Textile products regulations

These cover all textile products made up of not less than 80% weight of textile fibre. This therefore excludes most items where the textile is a minor trim or non-functional requirement, such as a textile trim on shoes or handbags. Some items are completely exempt, like egg cosies, watch straps and make-up bags. The regulations cover percentage compositions of textile blends, for example, 85% wool, 10% wool, 5% other fibres. All textile fibres which account for less than 10% of the blend can be described as 'Other fibres' but any others have to be described by percentage in descending order, that is starting with the most-used fibre. Any made-up fabric which accounts for less than 30% of a garment does not need to be labelled unless it is a main lining, not an interlining or wadding. The regulations also require that if there is a brand name, like Trevira for a generic textile product such as polyester, it should be placed immediately before the generic name.

Price marking (Bargain Offers Order 1979)

This introduces two legal requirements where retailers make comparisons with their own previous prices. Although retailers are required to have offered an item for sale for a consecutive period of not less than 28 days in the previous six months, this order adds that, where the previous price is quoted, at least one item must have been sold at that price, and that if that item was on sale at another branch or store of the same company, then it must be clearly stated.

Consumer Protection Act 1979

This Act makes retailers or suppliers who use an own-brand label liable to anybody who suffers as a result of that product being defective. Retailers are further liable for any defective product causing injury, unless they name their supplier or sources of supply. In addition this Act empowers the Secretary of State for Consumer Protection to issue regulations in relation to specific product categories, for example children's flame-resistant nightwear. Local authorities ensure that traders are complying with the relevant trading laws, and will investigate and help to uphold complaints. These departments are listed in local telephone directories under Trading Standards, Consumer Protection or Consumer Advice Bureaux.

Assignment

Make an illustrated brochure to demonstrate your understanding of the Sale of Goods Act 1979. Be sure to explain the following terms, possibly stating examples of goods that you have bought in the past:

a) merchantable quality
b) fit for the purpose
c) corresponding to description
d) getting a refund

The illustrations can be line drawings or pictures cut from magazines. The brochure can be photocopied and then distributed to family or friends. Make sure you fully understand the implications of the law before impressing it on others!

Chapter 9

THE EDUCATORS AND TRAINERS

Many readers of this book will already be employed in one or other aspect of the fashion business, whilst others may be considering what type of career opportunities there are, and how to embark on them. Whilst not intending to adopt the role of careers adviser, this chapter aims to give useful information and advice on how the prospective student should proceed.

There are four main categories of training course:

- university, polytechnic and college courses, full-time and part-time
- YT schemes
- trainee schemes with employers
- short courses

University, polytechnic and college courses, full- and part-time

City and Guilds

These are mainly courses in technical subjects, for example machine-knitting.

BTEC (and Scottish equivalents)

These courses lead to three different levels of qualification:

First Diploma – a first level qualification
National Diploma – post first diploma or post GCSE
Higher National Diploma – post national diploma or post A level

Higher education degrees

First degree, postgraduate diploma and Masters degree courses are available. Many of these courses specialise in one aspect of fashion, or fashion-related subject area, but more and more of these courses are now offering mixed subject fields or modular approaches to study so that you can pick and choose the component subjects which interest you. It is through this development that a lot of courses are now mixing business studies with fashion.

Look in public, school or college libraries for:

Which Degree?
Polytechnic Courses Handbook
Design Courses in Britain (Design Council)
Directory of Further and Higher Education (Longman)
Floodlight (Association of London Authorities – part-time courses in London only)
Local directories

Handbooks on higher education courses are also available from:

Art & Design Admissions Registry (ADAR)
24 Widemarsh Street
Hereford
HR4 9EP

PCAS (Polytechnics & Colleges of Higher Education)
PO Box 67
Cheltenham
GL50 3SF

UCCA (University)
PO Box 28
Cheltenham
GL50 1HY

Start thinking about the university, polytechnic or college course about a year before you actually want to start. Once you have an idea of what courses are available it is best to send well in advance for the university/polytechnic/college prospectus and detailed course information. Use this printed information as an aid to counselling, speak to as many people as you can, visit the university, polytechnic or college and take advantage of any open days, as this all helps to prepare you for an interview.

Access courses

Many universities, polytechnics and colleges now offer alternative access to their courses for adults, either by accrediting learning that has previously been acquired by the adult in the workplace and elsewhere (this is still a very new concept) or by offering preparatory access courses designed to prepare adults for the rigours of higher education. Many colleges and adult education institutes also offer courses for adults which do not lead on to higher education courses.

YT schemes

There are many types of YT scheme. They tend to fall into either the technical or the retail sphere. The best place to find out about what is available in your area is through the local Job Centre, but sometimes in the local press too.

Trainee schemes with employers

Many employers offer trainee schemes for students entering firms after GCSE, A Level and degree exams (or their equivalents). Examples of firms offering this sort of training are Miss Selfridge (retail), Burton Group (retail, buying and merchandising, etc.) and Marks & Spencer (all aspects).

These companies tend to be the larger retail-based organisations that can offer well-equipped in-house training suitable for all levels of employee. Contact such companies directly if you have a clear idea of where you want to go, or find out what is available in any particular year from careers advice services.

Many companies now offer training which is recognised as a National Vocational Qualification (NVQ).

Short courses

Many of these are available through commercial training consultancies and are often advertised in the trade press or through trade organisations, for example BSSA (British Shops and Stores Association), CAPITB (Clothing and Allied Products Industry Training Board) and the Clothing and Footwear Institute.

Some short courses or evening courses are also available at local universities, polytechnics and colleges.

SUGGESTIONS FOR FURTHER READING

This list is by no means exhaustive but many of these books and magazines helped me to formulate my own ideas; in addition, they are a source of both useful information and enjoyment.

MAGAZINES

DR The Fashion Business (weekly)
Fashion Weekly
Menswear (weekly)
Apparel (monthly)

BUSINESS REPORTS
Euromonitor
TMS
MINTEL
Retail Intelligence
Key Notes
Economist Intelligence Reports

BOOKS
Adburgham, A., *Shopping in Style*, Thames & Hudson, 1979
Cox, R. & Brittain, P., *Retail Management*, Pitman, 1988
Dale, G., *The Business of Retailing*, Hutchinson Educational, 1989
Everett, P., *You'll Never Be Sixteen Again*, BBC Publications, 1986
Fulton, V. (ed.), *Fashion Means Business*, Design Council Educational, 1988
Hebdige, D., *Subculture: The Meaning of Style*, Methuen, 1979
Haye, A. de la, *The Fashion Source Book*, MacDonald Orbis, 1988
Holdsworth, A., *Out of the Dolls' House*, BBC Books, 1988
Jarnow, J. A. & Judelle, B., *Inside the Fashion Business*, 2nd edn, Wiley, New York, 1974
Jones, D. & Franklin, C., *ID Bible: Every Ultimate Victim's Handbook*, part 1, Level Print, 1987
Howell, G., *In Vogue – Six Decades of Fashion*, Allen Lane, 1975
Knee, D. & Walters, D., *Strategy in Retailing: Theory and Application*, P. Allen, 1985
Ladbury, A., *Fabrics*, Sidgwick & Jackson, 1985
Laver, J., *A Concise History of Costume*, Thames & Hudson, 1983
Lurie, A., *The Language of Clothes*, Heinemann, 1981
Marly, Diane de, *The History of Haute Couture 1850–1950*, Batsford, 1980
Paola, H. de & Mueller, C. S., *Marketing Today's Fashions*, Prentice-Hall, 1986
Polhemus, T. & Proctor, L., *Pop Style*, Vermillion, 1984
Rennolds, C., *Couture: The Great Fashion Designers*, Thames & Hudson, 1985
Rodgers, D.S. & Gamans, L.R., *Fashion: A Marketing Approach*, Holt, Rinehart & Winston, 1983
Rouse, E., *Understanding Fashion*, BSP Professional, 1989

Tomlinson, A. (ed.), *Consumption, Identity and Style*, Routledge, 1990

Veblen, T., *The Theory of the Leisure Class*, Allen & Unwin, 1970

Watkins, J.E., *Fairchilds Who's Who in Fashion*, Fairchild, New York, 1975

Whiteley, N., *Pop Design: Modernism to Mod*, Design Council, 1987

Williams, K.C., *Behavioural Aspects of Marketing*, Heinemann, 1981

Wilson, E., *Adorned in Dreams*, Virago, 1985

Wilson, E. & Taylor, Y., *Through the Looking Glass*, BBC Books, 1989

Winters A.A. & Goodman, S., *Fashion Sales Promotion*, 6th edn, FIT, New York, 1984

York, P., *Modern Times*, Heinemann, 1984

ACKNOWLEDGEMENTS

The author and publishers are grateful to the following for permission to reproduce texts and illustrations. It has not been possible to identify sources of all the material used and in such cases the publishers would welcome information from copyright owners.

Mary Evans Picture Library for the photographs on p. 4; Popperfoto for the photographs on pp. 9 and 11 (hot pants and playsuit); Barnaby's Picture Library for the photographs on pp. 11 (leisure shorts with braces) and 12 (flapper); Camera Press for the photograph on p. 11 (baggy trousers); the Ronald Grant Archive for the photograph on p. 12 (crisis silhouette); Chris Moore for the photographs on p. 17; Pierre Cardin UK Ltd for the advertisement on p. 18; the SEHM Organisers / Promosalons UK for the advertisement on p. 20; Andrew Eccles Photography for the photograph on p. 26 (original) – first published in Shirley Kennedy, *Pucci: A Renaissance in Fashion* © Abbeville Press, New York; Express Newspapers for the photograph on p. 26 (copy); Pictorial Press for the photograph on p. 31; Mark Lally / *i-D Magazine* (photo Mark Lally, style Travis, model Barnaby) for the photograph on p. 36 (street fashion); John Birdsall Photography for the photograph on p. 36 (retail fashion); Assyst for the illustrations on pp. 41, 42; Lectra Systems Ltd for the photograph on p. 44 (top); Bullmer UK Ltd for the photograph on p. 44 (bottom); Lea Designs for the advertisement on p. 55; Richard Shops for the illustration on p. 59; Mintel International Group Ltd for the table on p. 67; *Elle* magazine for the illustration on p. 69; Levi Strauss (UK) Ltd for the Levi press release on p. 72; and Nigel French International / Clothing World for the article on p. 75.

INDEX